Ding Dong

Marc Camoletti and Tudor Gates

A Samuel French Acting Edition

SAMUELFRENCH-LONDON.CO.UK
SAMUELFRENCH.COM

Copyright © 2009 by the Estate of Marc Camoletti and
Drumbeat Productions Ltd
All Rights Reserved

DING DONG is fully protected under the copyright laws of the British Commonwealth, including Canada, the United States of America, and all other countries of the Copyright Union. All rights, including professional and amateur stage productions, recitation, lecturing, public reading, motion picture, radio broadcasting, television and the rights of translation into foreign languages are strictly reserved.

ISBN 978-0-573-11108-2

www.samuelfrench-london.co.uk

www.samuelfrench.com

FOR AMATEUR PRODUCTION ENQUIRIES

UNITED KINGDOM AND WORLD
EXCLUDING NORTH AMERICA
plays@SamuelFrench-London.co.uk
020 7255 4302/01

Each title is subject to availability from Samuel French,
depending upon country of performance.

CAUTION: Professional and amateur producers are hereby warned that *DING DONG* is subject to a licensing fee. Publication of this play does not imply availability for performance. Both amateurs and professionals considering a production are strongly advised to apply to the appropriate agent before starting rehearsals, advertising, or booking a theatre. A licensing fee must be paid whether the title is presented for charity or gain and whether or not admission is charged.

The professional rights in this play are controlled by Eric Glass Ltd, 25 Ladbroke Crescent, London W11 1PS.

No one shall make any changes in this title for the purpose of production. No part of this book may be reproduced, stored in a retrieval system, or transmitted in any form, by any means, now known or yet to be invented, including mechanical, electronic, photocopying, recording, videotaping, or otherwise, without the prior written permission of the publisher. No one shall upload this title, or part of this title, to any social media websites.

The right of Marc Camoletti and Tudor Gates to be identified as author of this work has been asserted by them in accordance with Section 77 of the Copyright, Designs and Patents Act 1988

DING DONG

Ding Dong was first produced at the Capitol Theatre, Horsham, in April 2005 under the title *Just Desserts!* with the following cast:

Bernard Marcellin	Giles Watlin
Jacqueline Marcellin	Sabina Franklyn
Marie-Louise	Anita Graham
Robert Regnier	David Callister
Barbara	Malandra Burrows
Juliette Regnier	Britt Ekland

Directed by Ian Dickens
Designed by David North
Production co-ordinator Caroline Burnett

CHARACTERS

Bernard Marcellin, businessman, late 40s
Jacqueline Marcellin, Bernard's wife, mid 30s
Marie-Louise, their maid, early 40s
Robert Regnier, Jacqueline's lover, about 30
Barbara, call girl, late 20s
Juliette Regnier, Robert's wife, about 30

SYNOPSIS OF SCENES

The action takes place in the Marcellins' luxurious duplex apartment in Montparnasse, Paris.

ACT I
SCENE 1 Mid-afternoon
SCENE 2 That evening

ACT II
SCENE 1 Immediately following
SCENE 2 Immediately following

Time — the present

Other plays by Tudor Gates
published by Samuel French Ltd

Ladies Who Lunch
Who Saw Him Die?

ACT I
SCENE 1

The living-room of the Marcellins' duplex apartment in Montparnasse, Paris. It is mid-afternoon

The room is spacious and luxurious and furnished with great taste. UC *curtained, sliding glass doors lead to a terrace overlooking the city.* UR *there is a staircase, below which a door leads to a hallway and the front door which cannot be seen.* R, *there is a mirror and a service bell with a string, and a table on which there is a phone and Bernard's diary. A door leads to a private study* DR. L *there are two doors leading to domestic offices, and* L *of these there is a well stocked drinks cabinet with glasses. There is a sofa with some cushions and a chair* C

As the Lights come up, Bernard is standing C, *thinking. He is stocky, like a peasant, but very well dressed. After a moment, he mimes his plan: playing Marie-Louise, the maid, as she opens the front door to let in a visitor, urging them to sit down and make themselves comfortable. The idea to get across is that Bernard is practising for a romantic assignment*

This is underlined by his guilty start as his wife, Jacqueline, enters from the top of the stairs. Jacqueline is in her mid-thirties, very elegant. She is dressed for going out. Bernard is older, by at least ten years. These people are rich

Bernard When d'you expect to be back?
Jacqueline (*checking her appearance in the mirror*) Depends on the traffic.
Bernard This time Saturday, everyone's travelling out of town, for the weekend. You'll be a while, won't you?
Jacqueline Don't fuss. I won't be late.
Bernard How late?
Jacqueline (*checking her hair in the mirror*) Eight, eight thirty. Depends how long Jean-Louis keeps me.
Bernard How long does it take to have your hair cut?
Jacqueline He's not a barber, darling. He's a stylist! (*Still checking*

herself in the mirror) You wouldn't understand. Anyway, I like to indulge myself.
Bernard You do, don't you?
Jacqueline I just like getting out of the house sometimes. And I saw a darling little cashmere jacket, so I might pop along to the rue de Passy —— (*Glancing at her watch*) Good lord, I'm late.

She moves towards the hall door. Bernard accompanies her

Bernard Oh! How terrible. What happens if you don't get there on time?
Jacqueline Don't ask. Jean-Louis would sulk for a month. I'll be all right if I leave right now.

She embraces Bernard. He holds on to her

Bernard Remember what I said about those mad Saturday drivers.
Jacqueline I'm always very careful, you know that. (*She pecks him on the cheek*) You'll be all right on your own, won't you?
Bernard I'll be fine. Don't worry about me. There's no need to hurry back.

Jacqueline beams at him

Jacqueline (*moving towards the front door*) You're such a darling. (*She blows him a kiss; as she goes*) See you.

Jacqueline exits

He stands in the hall doorway, watching her

Bernard (*calling*) Bye.

The front door closes. Bernard pauses for a moment, then goes to the middle of the living-room and returns to his thoughts. After a moment's pause, he moves to the terrace and looks down to the street to make sure Jacqueline has left. He comes back to the living-room, goes to the service bell, tugs at the string and then returns to the terrace

> Marie-Louise *enters from the* L *door, wiping her hands on the front of her apron. She is in her early forties probably, generous in build, an independent-minded country girl pressed into service – and she has never really come to terms with it*

Act I, Scene 1

Bernard is still standing US, *deep in thought. She looks around for a moment, not seeing him at first*

Marie-Louise (*noticing Bernard*) Oh, there you are.

Bernard comes back into the middle of the living-room. He pauses, still thinking

Bernard Marie-Louise ...
Marie-Louise (*cheerfully*) That's me.
Bernard My wife's gone to the hairdresser.
Marie-Louise Yes?
Bernard Her usual Saturday appointment. She goes every Saturday.
Marie-Louise Some people can afford it. I can't. Not on what I get.
Bernard (*affecting nonchalance*) She's always away for a couple of hours, right?
Marie-Louise At least.
Bernard Good.

Bernard stands there, lost in his thoughts for a moment. Marie-Louise observes him

Marie-Louise Have you done? I've forgotten what I came in for now.
Bernard Oh, yes. I'm expecting a visitor.
Marie-Louise Are you? When?
Bernard Soon. Now.
Marie-Louise While your wife's out?
Bernard Yes. (*Putting an arm around her shoulders*) I'm going to take you into my confidence, Marie-Louise.
Marie-Louise Oh?
Bernard Imagine Saturday was your day off ...
Marie-Louise What for?
Bernard Just for argument's sake.
Marie-Louise There's no argument so far as I'm concerned. My day off is tomorrow.
Bernard I know that but I want you to have it off today.

Marie-Louise looks at him intently. Her lips twitch

Marie-Louise (*not uninterested*) Have it off?
Bernard Yes.
Marie-Louise (*coyly*) I thought you had a visitor coming?
Bernard I have.
Marie-Louise You don't mean me ...

Bernard What?
Marie-Louise Me as well?

Marie-Louise gives him a saucy look which causes him to drop his arm as though he'd been scalded

Bernard As well as what? Just listen, will you?
Marie-Louise (*disappointed*) All right. I'm listening.
Bernard OK. (*He pauses to think*) A man is going to come here.
Marie-Louise (*surprised and shocked*) A man!
Bernard He has an appointment. At three o'clock.
Marie-Louise (*with cold disapproval*) I see. So?
Bernard But he doesn't know it.

Marie-Louise does a double-take. She is beginning to be concerned about her employer now

Marie-Louise (*encouragingly*) That's all right then. If he doesn't know, he won't come.
Bernard Well, he does know but he doesn't know it's with me, if you see what I mean ...
Marie-Louise (*after a pause*) A sort of male escort service?
Bernard (*exasperated*) His appointment is with my wife. Do you understand now?
Marie-Louise No.
Bernard Why not?
Marie-Louise Because she's just gone out.
Bernard That's right. He *thinks* he has an appointment with my wife. He doesn't *know* that his appointment is with me.
Marie-Louise (*as if finally comprehending*) Aah. He doesn't really know much at all, does he?
Bernard (*pleased with himself*) Damn right.
Marie-Louise He knows even less than I thought he did.
Bernard So, as he's expecting to meet my wife, he won't be expecting to meet me, right?
Marie-Louise I wouldn't like to say. He's as mad as a hatter, if you ask me. Or someone is.
Bernard (*ignoring her*) Just listen. The point is he won't hang around if he finds you here.
Marie-Louise Why? What's he got against me? I don't even know the man.
Bernard No, but my wife has told him you won't be here. That it's your day off.

Act I, Scene 1 5

Marie-Louise But it's not.
Bernard Don't let's go into that again. She wanted to let him know she'd be alone.
Marie-Louise I see. (*She doesn't see*) So there was just going to be the two of them.

Bernard nods

And she was supposed to be here?

Bernard nods

And now she's not?
Bernard At last! You've got it.
Marie-Louise You think so?
Bernard So, when this man rings the front doorbell ...
Marie-Louise Ye-es?
Bernard Well, I can't answer it, because he doesn't know I'm here.
Marie-Louise (*as comprehension dawns*) Aah.
Bernard (*spelling it out*) So who does that leave to let him in?
Marie-Louise I thought you said it was my day off?
Bernard I said *imagine* it's your day off.
Marie-Louise (*making out she understands*) Aah.
Bernard So, you open the door, let him in ...
Marie-Louise And then clear off?
Bernard Exactly.
Marie-Louise So I've got to act as though it's my day off, but it won't be?
Bernard Correct.
Marie-Louise (*sniffily*) I must say, you raised my expectations.
Bernard Never mind about that. So. (*Pointing a finger at her*) You invite this man in and tell him Madame will be home soon.
Marie-Louise And then I go out?
Bernard Yes.
Marie-Louise As if it's my day off?
Bernard Yes.
Marie-Louise With my best clothes on, and everything?

Bernard is delighted that she understands at last

Bernard Right! And then you come back in. (*He twirls his fingers*)

She nods sagely

Marie-Louise Round the back, through the service entrance?
Bernard Right. Then you take your clothes off.
Marie-Louise (*stiffly*) What exactly is this gentleman expecting of me?
Bernard (*pointing at her apron*) I mean you can go back to normal then.
Marie-Louise My day off's finished?
Bernard Right.
Marie-Louise Didn't last long, did it?
Bernard No. It was just a pretence. Thank heavens, you've got it at last!
Marie-Louise Oh, I've got it all right. (*She moves towards the service door; muttering*) I'm not sure what I've got ... (*As she goes*) But I've got it.

She exits, then comes straight back in again

You know it's three o'clock now, don't you?
Bernard Well get on!

Marie-Louise exits through the service door

Bernard pauses for a moment to consider his strategy, then he goes to the telephone and taps out a number. It rings but there is no answer. He listens a while, then puts down the phone. He looks around the room and mimes the scene he is trying to create: where Marie-Louise welcomes the guest

After a moment, the front doorbell rings, startling him. He almost answers it, then remembers and moves quickly towards the service entrance to call Marie-Louise

She anticipates him, almost knocking him over as she comes back into the living-room. She has removed her apron and is carrying a hat and handbag

Marie-Louise Just made it!
Bernard Right! Open the door, but wait 'til I'm gone.
Marie-Louise You're going out?
Bernard No. (*He moves towards the study door*) But I'm not here.
Marie-Louise Oh, right. (*She dons her headgear*) D'you like the hat? I thought it'd make it look as if I was really going out.
Bernard Very nice. Now, do you remember what you've got to say?
Marie-Louise Yes. Mostly nothing.

Act I, Scene 1   7

Bernard I'm relying on you, Marie-Louise. Don't let me down.

The front doorbell rings

> *Bernard places a finger to his lips and makes a hurried retreat to the study, through the door* DS

Marie-Louise takes a critical look at herself in the mirror and adjusts her hat. The doorbell rings again

Marie-Louise All right, all right, I'm coming. (*Moving to the hall door*) He's a bit impatient, isn't he?

> *Marie-Louise exits to open the front door*

(*Off*) Good-afternoon, monsieur.

> *Robert Regnier enters from the hall. He is thirty, maybe, slender in build, a bit of a dandy. He is carrying a bunch of flowers*

> *Marie-Louise follows Robert into the living-room, closing the hall door behind her*

Robert (*looking around uncertainly*) Thank you, madame.
Marie-Louise Mamsell.
Robert I beg your pardon?
Marie-Louise It's the hat.
Robert Hat?
Marie-Louise Makes me look older.
Robert Oh, I see. Yes.
Marie-Louise (*worried*) You think so too, do you?
Robert (*bewildered*) This is the, er, *Marcellin* house?
Marie-Louise Yes, and you've come to see Madame?
Robert (*relieved*) That's right.
Marie-Louise That's right. I was told you'll be expecting Madame … and that's about all I was told, really. To look after you when you came … Oh, and to tell you Madame is out but she'll be with you soon. Would you like to sit down?

Robert sits gingerly on the edge of a chair, still clutching his flowers

Robert Thank you.
Marie-Louise Of course, Madame would've answered the door if she'd been here. I'd have been gone as a rule, by now.
Robert Oh?

Marie-Louise That's why I've got my hat on. (*Holding up her handbag*) And my handbag.

Robert does not understand in the least the need for all this detail, but nods politely

Robert Well, don't let me keep you.
Marie-Louise No. (*She looks pointedly at her watch*) I really must go. So, if you're all right then, I'll get along.
Robert Please ... and thank you for staying.
Marie-Louise Madame should be here any time now. That's what I was told to tell you, anyway.
Robert Fine. Thank you.
Marie-Louise You won't be long without company, that's for sure.
Robert No. Thanks.

Robert politely rises as Marie-Louise moves reluctantly towards the hall door

> *Bernard pokes his head out of the study door, gesturing for Marie-Louise to leave*

Marie-Louise looks over Robert's head towards Bernard, querying what he wants of her

> *Bernard disappears and closes the study door*

Robert turns to see what Marie-Louise was looking at but sees nothing

Marie-Louise Right. Well. I'd better be off then. Because ... (*She opens the hall door*)
Robert It's your day off. I understand. *Au revoir*, madame.

Marie-Louise pauses in the doorway

Marie-Louise (*pained*) Mamsell. It's the hat that makes me look older.

Robert gestures a plea for forgiveness

> *Marie-Louise goes out the front door and bangs it behind her*

Robert rests the flowers on a side table. He takes a stroll around the room, looking out at the terrace and the view beyond. He comes back, spots the drinks cabinet and pours himself a glass of something. He sips at his drink and, full of himself, practises a few fancy dance steps

Bernard makes a noise, which Robert thinks comes from the floor above. He smiles and moves to the foot of the stairs

Bernard pops his head out from the study, watching Robert

Robert Yoohoo, Jacqueline? (*Coyly*) Are you hiding from me?
Bernard (*calling out with a high voice; muffling the sound with his hand*) Cooee.

Bernard goes back into the study, closing the door

Robert looks around. There is no one in sight. He correctly identifies the sound as coming from the study. Enjoying this little game, he picks up the bunch of flowers and moves towards the study door

(*Calling*) Come out, come out, wherever you are ...

As the door handle turns, Robert makes an exaggerated bow while holding out the bunch of flowers

The door opens and Bernard enters. He looks at the bunch of flowers

Bernard Yes?
Robert (*straightening up*) Oh my God.
Bernard Did you want something?
Robert Me? Nothing.

He stands there, flowers in one hand, drink in the other, his mind totally fuddled by the turn of events

Bernard Then why are you here?
Robert I've got the wrong address.
Bernard How do you know that? What's the right address?
Robert Er, number, er ...
Bernard What?
Robert (*thinking; desperately*) Monsieur Garden's apartment.
Bernard Monsieur Garden?
Robert Yes. (*With a little more confidence*) Monsieur Garden.
Bernard (*after a pause; suspiciously*) And you've brought flowers for Monsieur Garden?

Robert nods and smiles, holding the bunch of flowers towards Bernard, who makes an exaggerated show of starting away from him. Robert realizes he has goofed over this

Robert Yes, well, no, no. (*Floundering desperately*) They're for, er ...
Bernard For Madame Garden?
Robert (*thankfully*) Precisely. Yes.
Bernard Yes. And while you were waiting, you helped yourself to a drink?
Robert What? Oh yes, sorry. (*He hands Bernard his glass*) I'm afraid this was all a terrible mistake.
Bernard What was?
Robert Well, thinking this was Monsieur Garden's apartment, when it's clearly not.

Robert smiles and spreads his hands, seeking to share the ridiculousness of the mistake with Bernard. Bernard's face remains stony

Bernard How do you know it's not? How d'you know I'm not Monsieur Garden?
Robert (*still smiling*) But I know Monsieur Garden.
Bernard Oh really? I didn't get that impression when we first met.

Robert seeks to extricate himself again as Bernard waves his excuses away

No matter. In fact, I admit, I'm not Monsieur Garden. But, curiously enough, I was expecting you.
Robert (*bewildered*) Me?
Bernard Yes. (*Glancing at his Rolex*) And you're spot on time.
Robert Huh?
Bernard My wife told you to be here at three o'clock.
Robert Your wife!
Bernard Yes. She faxed you at the hotel. In the rue de Longchamps?
Robert Rue de Longchamps?
Bernard Do you always parrot everything people say to you? The place where you rent your studio apartment.
Robert Studio apartment?
Bernard There you go again. And, to make sure you got the message, she sent you a text. "Come to my place at three, et cetera." But I sent the message. (*He gets a mobile phone out of his pocket and holds it up*) On her mobile phone. (*He puts the phone back in his pocket*)
Robert I'm sorry?
Bernard What for?
Robert I didn't get a fax.
Bernard Then why are you here?
Robert Is this some kind of joke?

Act I, Scene 1

Bernard It's no joke for my wife. *She's waiting for you at your apartment. As you arranged.*
Robert Look, you must be confusing me with — I don't know who, but someone else. Forgive me, but enough is enough.
Bernard Exactly my feelings. And that's why I wanted to see you, Monsieur Regnier.
Robert Ah! That's the confusion. My name's not Regnier.
Bernard Yes, it is.
Robert No, it's not.
Bernard Yes, it is.
Robert Oh, no, it isn't.
Bernard Oh, yes, it —— (*He refuses to be drawn into this pantomime exchange*) Shut up! You are Robert Regnier. Occupation — other than philanderer — company director, with Plasticos. They're doing very well, aren't they?
Robert Well, yes, that's true — about Plasticos, I mean.
Bernard Everything I've said is true. I know all about it. Funnily enough, as the result of my car breaking down.
Robert What's that got to do with it?
Bernard I had to use my wife's Clio and I found a bunch of parking tickets, all for Saturdays between five and seven in the *rue de Longchamp* — which is not where she was supposed to be.
Robert I'm sorry. I can't see the connection.
Bernard Then you're thick! (*Menacingly*) Let me tell you something, Monsieur Regnier. I'm a very jealous man.
Robert (*placating*) I can see that.
Bernard Which is why I decided to follow my wife.
Robert (*trying to act like someone else*) That wasn't very nice.
Bernard Maybe not. (*Menacingly*) But it's not your place to tell me that, is it? Anyway, we all do what we think is right. And — to cut a long story short — I know you've been her lover for the past six months.
Robert This is just your imagination.
Bernard This is an unfortunate fact.
Robert No, no, these are wild assertions.
Bernard Do you think I wanted to find out what I did?
Robert They prove nothing!
Bernard They do for me. So don't argue. By getting you to come here, I'm going easy on you.
Robert But there's no reason to go easy, or anything else.
Bernard Would you prefer it if I rang your wife, Juliette? Told her?
Robert Er, no, that wouldn't be a good idea. She might not understand.

Bernard No. She might not. So stop denying it. Remember I know everything. (*Spitting out the word*) Facts!

Robert nervously decides to make the best he can out of a bad situation

Robert Er ... well, OK, look, if it's any consolation ... I feel terrible about this.
Bernard So do I.
Robert But what can I say? I promise you I'll never see your wife again.
Bernard Why not?
Robert Uh?
Bernard Don't you fancy her any more?
Robert Oh, yes. (*He doesn't quite know how to take this*) I think she's, er — sensational.
Bernard Isn't she just?
Robert (*trying to go along with him*) Fantastic!
Bernard Absolutely.
Robert (*warming to this line*) I'd even say, unique!
Bernard The perfect description.
Robert Exactly.
Bernard I'm delighted to see we share the same tastes.

There is a moment's dangerous silence. Robert, taking advantage of the recent conciliatory conversation, tries to resolve the situation

Robert It seems we do. Yes. But in view of the circumstances ... (*Gesturing expansively*) I defer, of course, to your prior claims — It's all over. Pouf!
Bernard (*dangerously*) Pouf?
Robert Absolutely. You have my word of honour. There.

Robert extends a hand of friendship. Bernard ignores it, looking at him. Robert's hand drops limply

Bernard You don't think that's just a little bit too easy?
Robert Well, I, er ... (*He gestures; confused*) You know ...
Bernard (*in a friendly, matter-of-fact tone*) I'm not sure I do. You sleep with my wife. Then, when I find out, it's "Oh, dear, sorry, won't do it again, bye-bye."
Robert Look, I mean no offence, but your wife made a choice of her own free will.
Bernard It takes two to tango?

Act I, Scene 1 13

Robert Exactly.
Bernard My wife is very emotional.
Robert Well, yes.
Bernard And so am I. I love her. She must never know that I know, and you must never let her know that I know.
Robert No. I mean, if you wish ...
Bernard I do. (*He smiles*) So, you see, I am being quite friendly about all this.
Robert I do see. Thank you.
Bernard All the same, there's no denying what's happened.
Robert I suppose not.
Bernard We can't repair the irreparable.
Robert Very true. You can't repair the irreparable.
Bernard I just said that.
Robert Sorry.
Bernard What's done is done.
Robert Yes. What's — yes.

Robert shrugs and sighs agreement with the sentiment

Bernard However, I do think I'm entitled to some compensation.

Robert looks at him

  For the injury I've suffered.
Robert (*unsure*) You're asking for money?
Bernard (*angrily*) What do you take me for — a pimp?
Robert No, no.
Bernard You think I'd rent her out, for money? Like a hire car? Fill her up, get a bit of mileage, then hand her back?
Robert No, of course not (*After a pause*) I don't understand what you want from me.
Bernard No. You're not too sharp on the uptake, are you? So I've been doing your thinking for you. And don't worry, I've found a solution.
Robert Oh, good. (*Cautiously*) I mean, I'm prepared to come to any reasonable arrangement.
Bernard Excellent. That's just the way I see it.
Robert (*puzzled*) What way?
Bernard You might even say there's more than one way — you've got a choice.
Robert You're going to let me choose?
Bernard Absolutely. An arrangement to your satisfaction. That is, from the two options I offer.
Robert (*relieved*) That's really very kind of you.

Bernard That's quite all right. You'll be able to thank me later.
Robert Of course. (*He offers his hand to Bernard*) Thank you.
Bernard Don't mention it.

They shake hands

I can't help it. Like I told you, I'm a very jealous person.
Robert I understand. Really. In fact, to tell you the truth, I'm a bit like that myself.
Bernard (*astonished*) No? You too?
Robert Absolutely. I know you wouldn't think it but, believe me, I'm terrible.
Bernard How terrible?
Robert Awful. I get absolutely furious if I think my wife, er ... (*Realizing he is walking into a trap, he changes track*) You can't imagine.
Bernard No one can imagine, can they, until it happens to them?
Robert (*changing the subject*) Anyway, about these arrangements?
Bernard Ah, yes. Let's see. (*Thinking*) The first possibility would be that I kill you.
Robert (*after a pause*) What did you say?
Bernard I said, that I kill you.
Robert (*trying to smile*) You're joking.
Bernard (*shaking his head*) I don't joke, monsieur. Not about things that are important to me. Let me tell you something about myself. I come from Marseilles. You know Marseilles?
Robert Er, no. I mean, I've never been there.
Bernard You should keep away. It is the murder capital of the country, you know that?
Robert Er, yes. I did see something on TV.
Bernard It is a tough place. To grow up there and survive, you have to be meaner than the next man. Do you follow me?
Robert Not quite.
Bernard It's kill or be killed. Your gang must be more ruthless than the opposition. Understand?
Robert You're a g-gangster?
Bernard I'm a businessman. I'm in the construction industry. We use a lot of concrete. It's a very useful material — concrete.
Robert Er, yes, I suppose so. I'm in, er, plastics.
Bernard Plastics don't have the same properties as concrete. You can't bury a corpse in it or use it to weigh a body down in the river.
Robert No. I suppose not.
Bernard I know what you do. And now you know what I do. So you'd better take me seriously.

Act I, Scene 1 15

Robert (*babbling*) But it would be a foolish thing to do, you'd be found out, you'd go to prison.
Bernard Why? I'd be nowhere near at the time. You don't think I'd dirty my own hands, do you? We Marseillaise stick together. I have friends. (*With emphasis*) Old friends. Who owe me favours.
Robert (*faintly*) You are joking, aren't you?
Bernard Does it sound as though I am?
Robert (*weak at the knees*) No.
Bernard Let me tell you something, my friend. I am one of those people who will always do what they say they will do.
Robert (*pleading*) But you can't be serious, can you? How could you talk about killing someone, just like that?
Bernard What d'you want me to do — burst into tears?
Robert But it would be a crime!
Bernard Of passion. In France, everyone would understand that. Even if I were involved personally.
Robert (*holding his head in his hands*) All right. You needn't say any more. I believe you.
Bernard Good. Now let us consider the relationship you have with my wife. I suppose I could say the relationship we have, couldn't I? You must understand I am a jealous man, I have to react, we Marseillaise have a code of honour. But don't worry. I will arrange it so that it is very quick. I would like to say painless but I can't guarantee that. But quick!

Bernard snaps his fingers. Robert is terrified

Robert But you don't know what you're doing.
Bernard Why do you say that?
Robert Because there would be an inquest. They would find out I was your wife's lover.
Bernard (*impatiently*) I've already told you. On the day of your, er, accident, I would be in Brussels. Or London. Yes, London. In the bar of the Ritz. I could take the Eurostar. I wouldn't be driving the truck that flattens you.
Robert (*after a gulp*) Truck?
Bernard Well, I say truck ... I leave this sort of thing to the experts. They know best, they choose their own time and method. I'd rather not know. (*Kindly, placing a comforting arm around Robert's shoulders*) But nothing's been decided yet. It all depends on you.
Robert Me?
Bernard (*jocularly*) You see, you're forgetting there's the second option.

Robert What's that?
Bernard That I sleep with your wife.

Robert breaks off from the embrace and backs away from Bernard

Robert No, come on ... Now I know you're crazy.
Bernard Look at it this way. The only thing you can give me in return for my wife is your own. Think of it as a code of honour.
Robert But I love my wife.
Bernard That didn't stop you from sleeping with mine.
Robert But it's not the same thing. My wife's always been faithful to me.
Bernard And how do you repay that? By cheating on her. Oh, no, justice demands a reversal of our roles. So your wife can deceive you with me and, thanks to her co-operation, I would no longer be faithful to my wife.
Robert You think that's just, do you?
Bernard It's equitable. The only honourable way. You're already suffering the same emotions I felt, and it hurt. A lot.
Robert You're right. It does. And that's why I refuse.
Bernard (*interested*) You refuse?
Robert It wouldn't have the same effect.
Bernard I think the fact that you refuse proves that it would.
Robert (*losing his temper*) You must be insane! Do you think I'm going to say to my wife, (*heavily sarcastic*) "Oh, darling, I want you to pop over to the Marcellins." (*As his wife*) "The Marcellins? I don't know them, do I?" (*As himself again*) "No, but they're a charming couple. Oh, and by the way, the husband wants to screw you."
Bernard (*after a pause*) Sounds all right to me. Except you couldn't, could you? Not without explaining why.
Robert Exactly! It's out of the question!
Bernard Aren't you being a bit hasty? It doesn't have to be so dramatic as you make out. All you have to do is make the introductions and then you can leave the rest to me.
Robert (*stiffly*) I don't think you realize the enormity of what you're suggesting.
Bernard Enormity?
Robert Yes.
Bernard When it concerns my wife, you seem to think it doesn't really matter, but when I mention yours, you make a great drama of it. Be logical.
Robert Logical? You're completely round the bend. If you care so much about your wife, why do you want mine?

Bernard I don't want you to think there's anything that's sort of perverted about this.
Robert (*scathingly*) Oh, no!
Bernard Not at all. It's a matter of honour. Where I come from, honour is everything. I need you to understand exactly the way I felt. That would be my compensation — perhaps even some consolation. But if you prefer the first option, I don't mind. It's up to you.

Robert is brought back to earth with a jolt

Robert (*hastily*) Wait a minute. Let me think.
Bernard (*glancing at his watch*) That's all right. You can have two minutes.
Robert What?
Bernard You heard me. Two minutes. No longer. Make your choice. (*He sets the second hand of his Rolex*)
Robert But you're being —
Bernard Unreasonable, I know. That's your view. (*He clicks the boss on his watch*) Countdown.
Robert (*babbling*) Right. OK. Sure. But —
Bernard No buts. You've got one minute and forty seconds left.
Robert Be reasonable!
Bernard We've already had this conversation.
Robert (*desperately*) Couldn't you think of some other way?
Bernard I've tried. And I can't. One twenty-five.
Robert (*edging towards the door*) And what if I just walk out, leave you standing there? Eh?
Bernard I won't stop you. I would take that as your answer. In your absence. One minute ten seconds.
Robert What d'you mean, in my absence?
Bernard Since we wouldn't be able to make arrangements for the second option, you would obviously have chosen the first. You do waste time, don't you? You've got less than a minute.
Robert Aren't we being far too hasty about this?
Bernard You've got forty seconds, Robert.
Robert To do what?
Bernard You know what. To give me your answer, to choose. Just over thirty seconds now. Leave, if you like. It was nice to have met you. Sad, though ...
Robert Sad?
Bernard That we'll never meet again. It's time, Robert. (*He studies his watch; after a pause*) Ten, nine —
Robert Right. Listen. OK.

Bernard What's OK? Four, three, two —
Robert (*screaming*) I agree!
Bernard To what?
Robert To sacrifice myself.
Bernard Well I'll be damned.
Robert (*bitterly*) Why so surprised?
Bernard I'm amazed.
Robert At what?
Bernard That you love your wife so much, you prefer to die.
Robert (*jittery*) I didn't say that.
Bernard You said you were going to sacrifice yourself.
Robert I am going to, damn it.
Bernard (*the penny drops*) Oh, I get it now. It's your ego you're sacrificing. Never mind the wife. (*After a pause*) Well, come on, tell me. I need to know what action I have to take.
Robert You are a monster!
Bernard Let's just say that to keep my wife, I'm capable of just about anything.
Robert Even to sleep with mine?
Bernard I'm prepared to make sacrifices too. So! No more messing about — do we have a deal?
Robert (*mumbling*) Yes.

Bernard cocks a hand to his ear

(*Louder*) Yes! (*Shouting*) Satisfied?
Bernard With what?
Robert (*spelling it out*) I will sacrifice my wife!
Bernard (*with barely concealed contempt*) Do you know something? I'm not really surprised.
Robert Aren't you?
Bernard Not at all. For someone like you, it was the only choice really, wasn't it? (*Adopting his friendly tone again*) Well now, since we see eye to eye, get on so well together, you must come and dine with us.
Robert What?
Bernard Well I'll need to be introduced to your wife. I mean, let's be civilized about this.
Robert (*after a gulp*) When?
Bernard Let's see ... (*He consults the diary on the side table*) No point in wasting time, is there? How about this evening?
Robert But what possible excuse can I give her for coming to your place on the spur of the moment?
Bernard You can tell her I'm an important business contact and that I've placed a big order with you. For the apartment block I'm developing.

Act I, Scene 1

Robert Oh yes, you're in construction. (*His business mind takes over momentarily*) Not much joy in that at the moment, is there? In fact, I feel sorry for you.
Bernard There's no need. The units were all pre-sold a long time ago. Straight off the plan.
Robert Oh? That was a bit of luck.
Bernard (*tapping the side of his nose*) Clever.
Robert Look, I just wanted to say —
Bernard You're not going to ask me to let you off, are you?
Robert No, no, of course not. (*He takes a notebook and a pen from his pocket; making notes*) But about your order, this building work?
Bernard OK. Since you're in the fibreglass business, you can supply me with, I don't know — say, five thousand metres of stair rail?
Robert (*brisk and businesslike*) Do you want it pre-formed or adaptable to your requirements?
Bernard How do you mean?
Robert Well, your rails. I'm going to need to have in stock exactly what you want. The fibreglass can be in any colour you choose.
Bernard What? Look, that's fine. But it's not really a question of my order, is it?
Robert (*stopping making notes; disappointed*) I thought I understood you were —
Bernard No, no. We're getting off the track with these rails. I'm just giving you the excuse you were looking for and it's a good one, if you can deliver the goods.
Robert (*brightening*) Well yes, but it's a fair quantity at short notice —
Bernard Not the fibreglass, you fool! It's your wife I want.

Robert is brought back to the harsh reality of the situation

Robert Ah yes, I'd forgotten. (*Putting away his notebook and pen*) But what if she doesn't want you?
Bernard Believe me, I always get what I want. If it's necessary, I'll feed her a few drinks.
Robert No, no, my wife is truly faithful. Even if you did get her drunk, it wouldn't make any difference. So then what?
Bernard Well then I'd have to fall back on the second option.
Robert What for? It wouldn't be my fault if she refused to sleep with you.
Bernard Don't try and shift the responsibility to your wife. (*Stabbing a warning finger*) You'd better hope she does come across.
Robert And what if she did?

Bernard Obviously, you wouldn't expect your wife to tell you about it. I'm sure she'd be a lot more discreet than you have been.
Robert Whatever ... how would I know? You could hardly expect me to trust you, could you?
Bernard That's your hard luck. But listen, so long as you don't see a big truck bearing down on you, you'll know heaven's on your side. Or at least, that it all went well.
Robert This is terrible.
Bernard No more for you than it was for me.
Robert Oh, yes, it is. You didn't know what was going on. Me, I'm just waiting for the worst to happen.
Bernard Well, that's only a moment's discomfort for you. I'm more concerned it won't be too painful for your wife.
Robert You're detestable!
Bernard Maybe. But I'm still the victim here.
Robert You're ... (*Struggling to find a word*) Vile!
Bernard Fine, if that's how you want it. Now then, to make all this believable, for the benefit of my wife as well as yours, we ought to call each other by our first names. I know we've only just met but people do, these days.
Robert Not in a situation of this kind.
Bernard I disagree. We need to create a friendly atmosphere.
Robert (*sarcastically*) Oh, sure. Let's pretend we're the best of friends, shall we?
Bernard All right then, we'll just stick to being polite, if that's what you want. But to keep up the pretence that you don't know my wife, it's essential that I formally introduce her to you.
Robert While you're trying to snog mine in a corner?
Bernard Why in a corner? I like my creature comforts. (*He clicks his fingers*) That's it! You know what would be a good idea? For you both to spend the night here.
Robert That's quite out of the question.
Bernard I suggested that in your own interest. I've got beautiful bedrooms upstairs. Connecting! So you see we might be able to get the result we want quite easily.
Robert You really like to put the boot in, don't you?
Bernard To you, yes. (*Pointing*) Remember, it was your choice.
Robert You arranged it so. I never really had a choice.

A noise sounds from above

Bernard Watch out, I think she's here.
Robert Who?

Act I, Scene 1   21

Bernard Jacqueline, of course. She's had enough of hanging about, waiting for you. (*Pointing to the study door*) Right, get in there! And don't come out under any circumstances. I'll call you when the coast is clear.
Robert Are you giving me orders?

We hear the front door open. Bernard pushes Robert towards the study

Bernard Right now, yes.
Robert (*groaning*) Oh, God.

Bernard shuts the study door in Robert's face

Robert exits. Jacqueline enters from the hall

Jacqueline (*calling*) It's me.
Bernard So I see. Back already?
Jacqueline (*exasperated*) I don't even want to talk about it. What an afternoon! God, the traffic!
Bernard I can imagine. It must be awful, having to wait about like that.
Jacqueline I've not been able to do a damn thing!
Bernard Oh, dear! And never even had your hair done?
Jacqueline (*looking in the mirror*) It's a mess, isn't it?

Bernard shrugs and gestures. He is not going to be caught like that

Bernard And you didn't get your cashmere jacket?
Jacqueline The traffic was so awful, I just had to forget about it. And it was hot, you know. I can always go during the week.
Bernard I don't know why you always want to go shopping on Saturdays.
Jacqueline (*changing the subject*) What about you?
Bernard What about me?
Jacqueline What have you been up to?
Bernard Oh, nothing much.
Jacqueline Uh, huh.

Jacqueline moves towards the study door

Bernard Where are you going?
Jacqueline In the study. I can't find my mobile phone.
Bernard No, wait. I've got something to tell you.

Jacqueline turns. There is a pause. She puts her hand on the study doorknob

Jacqueline Oh? What?
Bernard There'll be four of us for dinner this evening.
Jacqueline (*unenthusiastically*) Oh, yes?
Bernard It won't be too much of a hassle for you, will it?
Jacqueline (*moving back towards him*) Not for me, but have you warned Marie-Louise?
Bernard Not yet, but I'm going to.

Jacqueline looks in the mirror again and shakes her head

Jacqueline I'll have to go upstairs then, start getting ready. (*She moves back to the study*) But I must find my mobile.
Bernard (*quickly*) It's all right, I've got it. (*He produces it from his pocket*) I found it under a cushion. We haven't got long, you know?
Jacqueline Oh! (*She remembers the guests who are coming and forgets about the mobile; scolding*) I wish you wouldn't do this.

Jacqueline exits upstairs

Bernard smiles as he watches her disappear from view and then hurries to open the study door

Bernard Right. Move yourself.

Robert enters

(*Hurrying Robert towards the hall*) We dine at nine o'clock so you'd better be here by about eight thirty. Then I can start getting to know your wife while you pretend to get to know mine.
Robert (*protesting*) Look, is all this really —
Bernard Necessary? Yes. Our decision is irrevocable. I'm depending on you.
Robert Meaning what?
Bernard Meaning it's absolutely vital you come. Literally, because if you don't ...

Bernard's gesture is threateningly graphic. Robert, scared to hell, tries to retain his dignity

Robert Well, all I can say is ...
Bernard What?

Act I, Scene 1

Robert (*stepping into the hall*) You are a complete shit!
Bernard (*bundling him out*) Am I? What does that make you?

Robert and Bernard exit to the front door. Bernard comes back into the living-room. He pauses for a moment, then moves to the kitchen door and opens it

Bernard (*calling to Marie-Louise*) Hey! You!

Marie-Louise enters

Marie-Louise Now what?
Bernard Don't tell my wife about that gentleman coming here this afternoon.
Marie-Louise But I heard her come back, before he left.
Bernard Yes, but she didn't know he was here.
Marie-Louise I see. (*She doesn't see*)
Bernard But he'll be back before long for dinner.
Marie-Louise Dinner!
Bernard That's right. And, in front of my wife, you're to act as though you'd never seen him before.
Marie-Louise Right. But aren't you forgetting that I was just going out, on my day off, when he arrived?
Bernard That's right. And you did it very well.
Marie-Louise So, as I'd gone out, I couldn't have told your wife that I knew him, could I?
Bernard That's very good, Marie-Louise. Well done!
Marie-Louise (*entering into the conspiracy*) The trouble is, he saw me this afternoon, so he'll remember me when he comes.
Bernard Don't worry, he'll act as though he's never seen you before.
Marie-Louise Really? Everybody's seen everybody else, but nobody remembers anybody?
Bernard That's it. It's all quite simple.
Marie-Louise Oh, yes. It may be quite simple for you ——

Jacqueline comes down the stairs

Jacqueline (*to Bernard*) Have you told her there'll be four for dinner this evening?
Marie-Louise Four? But I thought ——
Bernard What did you think?
Marie-Louise Nothing. Nothing at all.
Bernard (*loudly*) Yes, there will be four of us. Have it ready for nine o'clock.

Marie-Louise OK, OK. There's no need to get excited.
Bernard (*stiffly*) I am perfectly calm.
Marie-Louise Well, good for you. But what about me? Dinner for four, at a moment's notice, for nine o'clock? Huh! I'm the one entitled to be in a tizzy!
Jacqueline You don't need to be. I'll give you a hand.
Marie-Louise Fine. If you'd like to take charge, that'd be even better.
Jacqueline I'll organize the menu, anyway.
Marie-Louise What does that mean? Look in the freezer?
Jacqueline (*to Bernard*) I'll be about ten minutes.

Jacqueline gestures Marie-Louise towards the door leading to the kitchen, and follows her. She notices the flowers and pauses

Jacqueline Oh, they're lovely!
Bernard What are?
Jacqueline (*picking up the flowers*) These flowers.
Marie-Louise Yes, they're nice. They're the ones —
Bernard Just a bunch of flowers.
Marie-Louise That's right. From —
Bernard The florist.
Marie-Louise Well, they don't come from the dry-cleaners, do they? No, that bunch is the one that —
Bernard I bought for you this afternoon. While I was out for a stroll. (*To Marie-Louise*) Didn't I?
Marie-Louise Absolutely!
Bernard Look, never mind about the flowers. Shouldn't you be getting on with the dinner?
Marie-Louise (*huffily*) Suits me!

Marie-Louise exits to the kitchen

Jacqueline (*admiring the flowers*) You are a darling.
Bernard If you say so.
Jacqueline I do, because it's true. (*Savouring the scent*) They're so beautiful!
Bernard Not bad, are they? I chose them for you myself.
Jacqueline I couldn't have chosen better. It shows how well you know me.
Bernard Yes, doesn't it?
Jacqueline I must put them in water, right away.
Bernard That's a good idea.

Jacqueline starts to move towards the kitchen door, then pauses

Act I, Scene 1   25

Jacqueline By the way, who are these people?
Bernard What people?
Jacqueline The ones who are coming to dinner. Who else?
Bernard (*vaguely*) Oh, them. (*He waves a hand*) A business connection to do with that development in Boulogne. It's a big order of handrails, for the staircases.
Jacqueline I see. Should be a fun evening.
Bernard Well, you know, they're all the same, aren't they, business meals?
Jacqueline Tell me about it.
Bernard I know. Anyway, to brighten up the evening, I told him to bring his wife. At least you two can have a chat while we're arguing prices.
Jacqueline Is she nice?
Bernard I hope so. But I can't say, really. I've never met her. But I've got to know him quite well.
Jacqueline Couldn't you have chosen some other time to discuss your handrails?
Bernard I'm afraid not. It's a matter of urgency, you see. And this chap can get me exactly what I want.
Jacqueline Has he got a monopoly then?
Bernard He seems to think he has, at least, for what I specifically want. He's the only person in Paris who can get it for me.
Jacqueline But what has he got that you can't get elsewhere?
Bernard Ah. You may well ask.
Jacqueline I *am* asking.
Bernard (*tapping the side of his nose*) Expertise. It's all to do with fibreglass.
Jacqueline (*bored*) Oh. (*She starts to go; remembering*) What's his name, anyway?
Bernard Er, I can't remember ... Gustav?
Jacqueline I thought you knew him quite well?
Bernard Yes, but we only met recently.
Jacqueline Gustav? That's Swedish, isn't it?
Bernard Yes, but he's not Swedish. In fact, his name's Robert. I've just remembered.
Jacqueline Well that's an improvement on Gustav.
Bernard Robert's a nice name, isn't it?
Jacqueline It's all right. What about his wife?
Bernard Oh, I've no idea.
Jacqueline You're hopeless. He must have mentioned her name.
Bernard I don't think so. Does it matter?
Jacqueline Well, if one's trying to make the conversation a little friendlier than "Monsieur, Madame" — yes it does.

Bernard Well, I'm sure he'll introduce her by name.
Jacqueline That would help.
Bernard I don't see the problem. It makes no difference to me what her name is. The point is, he says she's very nice. (*Rubbing it in*) In fact, the way he talks about her, they seem very much in love.
Jacqueline (*drily*) How long have they been married?
Bernard He didn't say. Actually, he's pretty boring. I just hope she's not.
Jacqueline Yes, well. I'd better go and see what we can dig up for the meal. (*She heads towards the kitchen*)
Bernard (*referring to the flowers*) What about these? You were going to put them in water.
Jacqueline (*coming back*) I sometimes think I'd forget my head if it wasn't screwed on.
Bernard (*presenting the flowers to her*) I wouldn't say that. (*Making it sound like a compliment*) I'd say you always know exactly what you're about.
Jacqueline (*smiling*) Most of the time, anyway.

Bernard holds the kitchen door open for Jacqueline

Jacqueline exits

Bernard But not always. (*He goes to the phone and dials; listening*) Answerphone. (*After a pause; into the phone*) Hello, Robert. Bernard Marcellin. Just confirming your invitation to dinner this evening at my place. You and, of course, your charming wife. About eight thirty, then. Fifteen rue St Michel. Au revoir. (*He hangs up; to himself*) Just so you don't try to leave her at home.
Jacqueline (*off; calling*) Bernard.

Bernard smiles then shoots his cuffs

Bernard Coming, my dear.

He moves towards the kitchen door

The Lights fade to Black-out

Scene 2

The same. That evening

The terrace is now a sparkling backdrop, reflecting the lights of Montparnasse, and the flowers now stand in a vase on the side table

Act I, Scene 2

The front doorbell rings

Marie-Louise enters from the kitchen and goes to the hallway to answer the door. She is not wearing an apron and looks smart in a dark dress

Marie-Louise (*off; opening the front door*) Good-evening.
Robert (*off*) Good-evening. We are expected.

Marie-Louise leads the way into the living-room. Robert follows

Marie-Louise That's right. For dinner. You're a bit early. It's not half-past eight yet.
Robert It's the time Monsieur Marcellin told me. (*Addressing the hallway; to Barbara*) Come in, my dear, come in.

Barbara enters the living-room. She is stunning, but a bit tarty. In her late twenties maybe. She is not as at ease in society as Robert is

Barbara Thank you. (*Holding out her hand to Marie-Louise*) Good-evening, Madame.
Marie-Louise (*accepting her hand; surprised*) Good-evening, Madame.
Robert No, that's not Madame Marcellin. (*He takes off his coat and hands it to Marie-Louise*) Here.
Barbara But I thought ... (*To Marie-Louise*) I'm so sorry.
Marie-Louise That's all right. I left my apron off, that's all. Funny the difference it makes, isn't it? (*Nudging Robert*) Surprised to find me here?
Robert No. (*Helping Barbara off with her coat*) Why should I be?
Marie-Louise Well, because this afternoon, I told you it was my day off.
Robert What about it?

Robert hands Barbara's coat to Marie-Louise, double-taking at the very brief minidress Barbara is wearing

Marie-Louise I had to come back, didn't I? Because of this dinner. So really, I never had a day off.
Robert (*without interest*) Oh, I see.
Marie-Louise So, as I'm back doing things, what can I do for you? (*To Barbara*) A drink maybe?
Barbara (*smiling*) Let me see ... I think I'd like a Manhattan.
Marie-Louise Certainly. (*Thinking*) What is that?
Barbara It's an American drink. A Manhattan.
Marie-Louise How do you spell that?

Robert Never mind, let's not go into that now.
Barbara But ——
Robert (*to Marie-Louise*) She won't have anything to drink.
Marie-Louise I see. What about you?
Robert No. Nothing.
Marie-Louise Not even something I know how to spell? Then I can look it up, see?
Robert No.
Marie-Louise Oh. All on the wagon, are we?
Robert For now, yes.
Marie-Louise Up to you. But don't let not having a drink stop you from making yourselves comfortable. I'll let them know you're here.
Robert Thank you.

Marie-Louise exits to the kitchen

Barbara I really wanted to have something.
Robert Later. We're not here for that.
Barbara Well, I know, but if someone politely offers me a drink ...
Robert (*tetchily*) Why did you have to ask for something so outlandish?
Barbara (*defensively*) I thought it was the "in" thing.
Robert Well, it's not.
Barbara It is on the telly. It's what ladies ask for on American TV.
Robert Perhaps. But not here.
Barbara All those American series. If anyone asks: "What'll you have, babe?", it's always a Manhattan. Or sometimes a dry Martini. But I can never understand how a drink can be dry. Makes no sense, does it?
Robert We're not in America, we're in France. A civilized country. And we're not on TV.
Barbara (*dismally*) I know that.
Robert So behave yourself. (*Looking her up and down*) And what on earth is that you're wearing?
Barbara You said, a little cocktail dress.
Robert Yes, I did but I didn't mean that little. That's not a mini, it's a bikini. But never mind that now. Listen, Barbara, try to remember what I told you. I don't want anything to go wrong.
Barbara It's not that difficult. I've only got to turn him on.
Robert (*looking around; lowering his voice*) Yes, but only a little bit, no more. Don't make him come on too much.
Barbara That's easier said than done.
Robert Don't worry, it'll work. Attract him as much as you like, but don't throw yourself at him.

Act I, Scene 2

Barbara Well, that's up to him, isn't it?
Robert What do you mean?
Barbara That's what I'm here for, you said so yourself. Make up your mind.
Robert I've told you. However strongly he comes on to you, don't give in. Defend yourself. Resist him. But not too much.
Barbara I see. Just as much as it takes. How much does it take? I don't have a lot of experience at this, you know? I mean, I do the other way round ...
Robert (*impatiently*) Surely you can see the problem we have? He knows that my wife, Juliette, is faithful to me. And if he realizes you're not my wife, then I'm in for the chop. I told you, he's a madman.
Barbara No, I don't think you did. Thanks very much.

Before the argument can continue, they are interrupted

Bernard enters from the study

Bernard Ah, I thought I heard the door.
Robert Yes. (*Putting an arm around Barbara's waist*) Here we are.
Bernard Good, good. (*He glances at Barbara approvingly, though perhaps his eyebrows lift a fraction*) I'm delighted.
Robert We're delighted to be here — as *arranged*.
Bernard (*approaching Barbara*) Well that's good news. (*Aside; to Robert*) For you.
Robert Darling, may I introduce you to Monsieur Marcellin. Bernard.
Barbara Good-evening.
Bernard I'm so happy you've come.

Bernard takes Barbara's hand and bends low to brush it with his lips

Barbara (*impressed*) Me too.
Bernard I must say, she really is quite lovely.
Robert I told you so.
Barbara Please. You're making me blush. Both of you.
Bernard I'm sorry, I can't help it. I'm the kind of man who has to say right out whatever he thinks. I'm very blunt, very straightforward, aren't I, Robert?
Robert Er, yes, er ... he doesn't mince words.
Bernard No. That's me, in all my business dealings. Your husband knows that.
Robert Definitely.
Bernard That's how people understand I mean what I say. (*To Robert*) Right?

Robert Right.
Bernard Fine. (*To Barbara*) Hasn't anyone offered you a drink yet? What would you like? Champagne? Whisky?
Barbara Could I have a Manhattan?
Bernard Sorry?
Barbara A Manhattan.
Bernard (*doubtfully*) Well, we're bound to have vermouth but I'm not sure about the bourbon.
Robert Don't worry about it.
Bernard No, if that's what the darling girl wants ...
Robert What it is — her parents used to stay in America a lot. She picked up the habit as a child.
Bernard Of drinking bourbon?
Robert Yes — I mean, no. She got used to seeing that kind of thing being drunk.
Barbara Just like they do in the TV series. You know, like *Friends*.
Bernard Ah.
Barbara Or *Sex and the City*?
Bernard Aah.
Robert And when she grew up, the habit kind of stuck with her.
Barbara That's it. I really like a Manhattan.
Bernard Then, if it's at all possible, you shall have one. And what's more, I will join you. (*He moves to the drinks cabinet; looking at it*) Now let's see ... Ah, here we are — vermouth, yes, I have some. (*He gestures desolation to Barbara*) But bourbon, — no. Whisky, malt, even rye ...
Robert (*to Bernard; winking surreptitiously*) When she drinks too much, she loses all self-control. Then I have to keep a careful eye on her. So champagne will be fine. (*To Barbara*) Won't it, darling?
Barbara OK.
Bernard Are you sure?

Barbara smiles at Bernard, who rings the nearby service bell to summon Marie-Louise

(*To Robert*) And what about you? Whisky, old chap?
Robert That will be fine. Old chap.

Marie-Louise enters from the kitchen

Marie-Louise You rang?
Bernard Yes. I don't suppose you know whether we've got any bourbon anywhere?
Marie-Louise Any what?

Act I, Scene 2   31

Bernard Bushmills? Jack Daniels? Wild Turkey?
Marie-Louise Why would I have a wild turkey?
Bernard It's a kind of whisky, used for making cocktails.
Marie-Louise What am I, a barman now, as well?
Bernard Never mind. Just bring in the champagne and some glasses.
Marie-Louise (*as she goes; grumbling*) At least with that I know what it is.

Marie-Louise exits to the kitchen

Bernard (*to Barbara*) I apologize for Marie-Louise. I hope you don't mind too much.
Barbara About Marie-Louise?
Bernard (*with great charm*) About her, about the Manhattan. But mainly for having dragged you out at such short notice.
Barbara Not at all, monsieur.
Bernard Come on now, you must drop that.
Barbara What?
Bernard We know each other too well — or I hope we will — you must call me Bernard.
Barbara Oh, right.
Bernard (*to Robert*) You don't mind, do you, old chap?
Robert Not at all. Old chap.
Bernard (*to Barbara*) There you are, you see. So, I am Bernard and you are … ?
Barbara I'm Ba ——
Robert Juliette!
Bernard Juliette!
Barbara Juliette.
Bernard Ah! Named after the famous lover.
Barbara Was I?
Bernard It could be. Such a sad story, though. Juliette and her little Romeo. (*To Robert*) Wasn't it?
Robert I suppose so. In the end.
Barbara What happens?
Bernard He dies. Tragic. But let's not think about such things. We're here to enjoy ourselves. And perhaps talk just a little business. What do you say, Bobby? You don't mind me calling you that, do you?
Robert (*he does mind*) No. Not at all, Bernie!

Both men laugh without humour

Marie-Louise, still aggrieved, enters from the kitchen with an ice bucket and a bottle of champagne. She wears an apron now

Marie-Louise Messieurs. Madame.
Bernard Thank you.
Marie-Louise (*setting down the ice bucket*) Shall I serve?
Bernard No, that's all right. I'll see to it.
Marie-Louise You're sure now? Because as well as getting the drinks and the dinner, not to mention everything else —
Bernard No, that's fine, thanks.
Marie-Louise I could always stick a broom up my apron and give the floor a sweep?
Bernard (*pointedly*) Thank you, Marie-Louise.

Marie-Louise flounces out to the kitchen

Bernard pours and hands a glass of champagne to Barbara

Bernard There.
Barbara Thank you.
Bernard (*raising his glass to her*) To the beautiful Juliette. (*To Robert; meaningfully*) Good health.
Robert I'll drink to that.

Jacqueline enters, beautifully dressed. She poses for a moment at the top of the stairs. She has not so far seen Robert but she is already starting down the stairs, hand held out in greeting, as Bernard speaks

Bernard (*moving to greet Jacqueline*) Ah good. Here she is at last. Darling, do come and meet my friend. (*He grabs Robert and pushes him to the foot of the stairs*) Robert. (*He pauses for dramatic effect*) Regnier.

Jacqueline suddenly sees who it is and completely loses her footing. She staggers down the stairs and almost falls. Bernard allows Robert to catch her as Barbara gasps. Robert, having straightened out Jacqueline, bows and steps back. Jacqueline glances with horror from Robert to Barbara and then back to Robert. Desperately striving to regain her composure, she holds out a hand

Jacqueline (*regally*) How do you do. So pleased you could come.

Bernard smiles with satisfaction

The Lights fade to Black-out

ACT II
Scene 1

The same. Immediately following

Jacqueline (*to Barbara*) So pleased to meet you.
Barbara (*shaking Jacqueline's hand*) Good-evening.
Robert Er ... how do you do, madame.
Bernard Oh, lighten up, old chap. (*To Jacqueline*) I know you haven't met before but we don't have to be that formal, do we?
Jacqueline (*faintly*) Er ... no.
Bernard Exactly. None of this monsieur and madame business all the evening. So, Juliette and Robert — this is my wife Jacqueline.
Robert (*extending his hand*) Delighted, er ... madame.

Jacqueline glares at Robert and gives him a perfunctory handshake

Bernard (*to Jacqueline*) What would you like to drink, darling?
Jacqueline Some champagne, I think.
Bernard (*pouring Jacqueline a glass and handing it to her*) Absolutely. Let's celebrate.
Jacqueline Thank you.

Jacqueline drinks the whole glass of champagne and hands Bernard her empty glass for a refill. She realizes everyone is looking at her as though she is an alcoholic

(*Weakly*) Hot, isn't it? Makes one thirsty.
Bernard (*enjoying himself*) Right. Here we are.

Bernard pours and hands Jacqueline another drink. She takes it, resisting the temptation to knock it back again. There is a moment of silence as each regards the other

Robert (*weakly*) Yes. Here we are. (*As a diversion, he points towards the terrace*) I bet you have a jolly good view from there.
Jacqueline Yes, it's very nice.
Bernard Better than that. It's stunning. (*To Barbara*) Don't you think so, my dear?

Barbara Yeah. Stunning.
Bernard (*to Robert*) You don't know this part of Paris, then?
Robert No, no, not at all. (*Overdoing it*) Never been here before.
Bernard Well, you must take a look around. It's an old building I've completely re-developed, keeping the top two floors and this roof terrace.
Robert Ah. A kind of maisonette.
Barbara In America, they call it duplex. (*Enjoying the word*) Duplex.
Jacqueline (*recovering her poise; to Bernard*) Why don't you take — Juliette? ——

Robert nods. Bernard nods. Barbara looks around blankly

— on a guided tour?
Bernard (*with pleasure*) If Juliette would like that?
Barbara (*to Robert; remembering she's his wife*) Can I?
Robert But of course, since Madame, er ...
Bernard (*tutting reproof*) Jacqueline.
Robert Sorry, yes, er ... since Jacqueline has been kind enough to suggest it.
Bernard Right. (*Beaming at Jacqueline and Robert*) And while I'm doing that, it will give you two the chance to get to know each other, won't it?
Jacqueline (*directing a steely glance at Robert*) Yes. It will.
Bernard (*to Juliette*) Right. Come along, Juliette. I think the best place to start would probably be my study. (*Leading Juliette to the study; to the others*) We won't be long. Help yourself, old chap. Your glass is empty.
Robert Oh, right ... thanks.

Bernard shows Barbara into the study, closing the door behind him

Jacqueline immediately turns to Robert

Jacqueline (*fiercely*) What the hell are you doing here?
Robert Who? Me?
Jacqueline Is there someone else?
Robert I was invited for dinner.
Jacqueline Don't play the fool with me.
Robert You'll soon find out if I'm playing the fool — your husband knows!
Jacqueline Knows what?
Robert About you — me. (*Making it clear*) Us!

Act II, Scene 1   35

Jacqueline You're joking!
Robert I'm not. He knows everything.
Jacqueline How do you mean, everything?
Robert I mean where we meet, which days, what time and where, how long we've been seeing each other — everything there is to know, he knows!
Jacqueline But he can't!
Robert Well, he does!
Jacqueline Are you certain?
Robert Of course I am. He told me himself. Here.
Jacqueline Here? I don't believe you. When? What did you say?
Robert What could I say? I came with some flowers for you. (*Pointing at the vase of flowers*) There!
Jacqueline It was you who bought the flowers?
Robert That's right.
Jacqueline But my husband said he'd bought them.
Robert Well, he would, wouldn't he? Damn cheek, though.

Marie-Louise enters hurriedly from the door leading to the kitchen

Jacqueline What do you want?
Marie-Louise Me? Nothing. But ever since you got back, I've been asking if it's OK to get the dinner on, and you keep telling me, later.
Jacqueline My mind's on other things.
Marie-Louise Well, it's up to you. But I really ought to get started.
Jacqueline (*distractedly*) What are we having?
Marie-Louise There isn't any soup.
Jacqueline I didn't ask you what we're not having. I asked you what there is.
Marie-Louise Well, there's sardines, mackerel, or you can have grilled sausages?
Jacqueline (*to Robert*) What would you like?
Robert (*distractedly*) Makes no difference to me. I'm not hungry.
Jacqueline Oh, serve whatever you think best.
Marie-Louise (*going to the kitchen; grumbling*) Right. No skin off my nose. Sod the sausages, it'll be either mackerel or sardines. I'll toss for it.

Marie-Louise exits to the kitchen

Jacqueline, still totally perplexed, turns back to Robert

Jacqueline I still don't understand how you came to be here while I was traipsing around rue de Longchamp.

Robert I came because you told me to come.
Jacqueline You're dreaming!
Robert Don't you see? Your husband sent me a text message, in your name. It said: "Come to my place instead. Same time. I'll be alone."
Jacqueline Oh my God!
Robert Imagine how I felt! I rush over here and bump right into him. I try to make excuses, but it's pointless. He tells me in a very matter-of-fact way that he knows the two of us are sleeping together!
Jacqueline You mean he knows and doesn't mind?
Robert Far from it! (*He breaks off as he sees Barbara and Bernard*)

Barbara comes in from the terrace, followed by Bernard

Bernard Yes, the terrace goes right round. All the rooms on this floor lead on to it. So it's very easy to get in and out, if you see what I mean.
Barbara Yes, it's very well laid out.
Jacqueline (*resuming her mask*) You like it, then?
Barbara Oh, definitely. I think it's super!
Jacqueline Perhaps you should show her the upstairs?
Bernard If you like. Jacqueline has her boudoir up there and there are four bedrooms, all en suites.
Robert Yes, you should take a look. We've been talking about decorating. The bedrooms might give you some ideas.
Barbara (*smiling brightly; to Bernard*) OK. Let's go!

Bernard indicates the staircase. As Barbara starts up it, Bernard follows

Bernard (*to Robert*) Please, have another drink. Help yourself.
Robert I'm fine, thanks.
Bernard Your glass is empty again. (*To Jacqueline*) Give him one, darling.
Jacqueline Of course, darling.

Bernard and Barbara exit upstairs

Jacqueline looks up the stairs, checking they have gone, then turns to Robert

Jacqueline (*fiercely*) But as soon as you were certain that he really did know, you should have told him you'd end the affair — immediately!
Robert That's just what I did — immediately! Unfortunately, it didn't make any difference.

Act II, Scene 1   37

Jacqueline How do you mean?
Robert I mean, that wasn't sufficient to repair his self-respect, or something like that, on account of the suffering that we'd caused him.
Jacqueline What suffering?
Robert You know ... (*Gesturing delicately*) You ... with me.
Jacqueline Oh. That. Well?
Robert He's demanding compensation!
Jacqueline You're lucky then. He can be very tough when he wants to. He's a killer. You got off lightly.
Robert You think so, do you? Well, that's just what happened. He threatened to kill me!
Jacqueline What?
Robert You heard!
Jacqueline Oh, come on, there's no need to panic. I know him. He wouldn't ... (*Thinking*) Well, not personally, anyway —
Robert No, he wouldn't! It'd be someone else driving the truck!
Jacqueline What truck?
Robert It's too complicated to explain. But the fact is, he's determined to have me killed! Because of you!
Jacqueline (*touched*) Does he really love me so much? Does he feel so desperately in need of revenge?
Robert Well, if you put it like that, yes.
Jacqueline Put it like that? That's what I call true love!
Robert You call it what you like. You haven't heard the alternative he gave me.
Jacqueline What?
Robert That he should sleep with my wife!
Jacqueline (*with a complete change of attitude*) Bastard! That's disgusting!
Robert Yes, it is. But, from my point of view, better than dying. So, now you know why I'm here. He forced me to accept the invitation to dinner so he could get to know my wife.
Jacqueline And you just handed her over?
Robert Well, it was that, or the other.
Jacqueline By the way, your wife's changed a lot.
Robert What d'you mean? You don't even know her.
Jacqueline No, but I saw her a few months ago, while I was waiting for you. You were coming out of the cinema.
Robert Yes, but you can't really call that knowing her. Just seeing her for a few seconds. (*He pauses*) In a crowd of people.
Jacqueline Yes, but I was taking notice. I remember thinking how petite she was.

Robert Obviously, things look smaller in the distance.
Jacqueline I was just across the street. (*Musing*) She looked smaller.
Robert Probably wearing flat heels.
Jacqueline I particularly remember her eyes. They were very bright.
Robert Reflection of the light. She wears contact lenses.
Jacqueline And her hair was quite different.
Robert It's always different. (*Confidentially*) She likes wearing wigs.
Jacqueline And her face was quite plump.
Robert Absolutely. Too plump. I told her. That's when she went on a diet.
Jacqueline She's dieting?
Robert Yes, she wants to reduce her figure too. You'd never believe how complicated it is. Massages with compresses of herbs. Incredible how it reduces fat — 'specially on the face. And then she uses those herb poultices. They brighten the whole complexion. So it's not surprising she looks different, is it, if you take account of the flat heels, the wig, the contact lenses, the massage ——
Jacqueline The herb poultices?

Robert spreads his hands

Shut up, Robert! Admit it, that's not your wife.
Robert She is, I swear.
Jacqueline Do you want me to scream?
Robert No! (*Glancing anxiously up the stairs*) Please! Let's stay calm about this.
Jacqueline If you want me to stay calm, then stop lying.

Marie-Louise bustles in from the kitchen, carrying something that can't quite be seen

Marie-Louise Oh well. That's settled.
Jacqueline What?
Marie-Louise The mackerel won.
Jacqueline Oh, good. Thanks for telling us. Is that all?
Marie-Louise No. When should I put the next course in?
Jacqueline What are we having?

Marie-Louise displays two cartons of frozen food

Marie-Louise A blanquette of veal or lamb stroganoff.
Jacqueline (*to Robert*) Which would you prefer?
Marie-Louise He's not hungry.

Act II, Scene 1   39

Robert I'm not hungry.
Jacqueline All right. Do whatever you think best.
Marie-Louise (*as she goes; grumbling*) Right! I'll have to toss up for it then, which one to defrost!

Marie-Louise exits to the kitchen, balancing the frozen food cartons

Jacqueline I'm warning you! I shall scream! And everyone will hear! (*She throws back her head and opens her mouth*)
Robert No! All right! I'll tell you!
Jacqueline Well?
Robert Yes, you're right. She's not my wife.
Jacqueline I told you that. What I want to know is who she is and what she's doing here.
Robert Look, the problem's this — Juliette is entirely faithful, so where does that leave me? I know your husband would never get anywhere with her. But with this girl ... (*Appealing desperately*) I did it to save my life!
Jacqueline No, you didn't. You did it to save your wife.
Robert No, yes — both! What choice did I have?
Jacqueline So you thought you'd trick him into sleeping with a whore?
Robert As a matter of fact, she comes from a very good family.
Jacqueline Don't make me laugh. How d'you know, anyway?
Robert (*quickly*) Someone told me. A very reliable source.
Jacqueline I'll bet. But it doesn't stop her sleeping with men for money.
Robert Well that's right. She's a sort of an escort. And that's why I —
Jacqueline You! You only think about yourself!
Robert (*exasperated*) Well, I must admit, I am thankful to be still alive!
Jacqueline You see? You're totally self-centered!

Marie-Louise enters brusquely

Marie-Louise Right, that's it. All sorted.
Jacqueline What?
Marie-Louise You're going to have the stroganoff.
Jacqueline Yes? Fine! Did you have to interrupt, just to tell us that?
Marie-Louise (*astonished and offended*) Oh, right, excuse me! In fact, pardon me for living! (*As she goes; loudly*) For some people, you can't do anything right!

Marie-Louise exits to the kitchen

Jacqueline So, that's all I'm worth, is it?
Robert What?
Jacqueline To be compensated for by a substitute!
Robert How could I have done anything else?
Jacqueline Your wife is too good for my husband, but this prostitute's all right?
Robert She's more of a call girl, really. Quite classy. I don't know what you're complaining about! What d'you want, to be an accomplice in my murder?
Jacqueline It would serve you right!
Robert For what?
Jacqueline Sleeping with another man's wife!
Robert Oh? You had absolutely nothing to do with it, I suppose?

Jacqueline is about to reply when they hear Bernard and Barbara coming down the stairs, chuckling together

Barbara gives Bernard a coy shove as they descend the stairs

Barbara Oh, Bernard! Those bedrooms! They're awful!
Jacqueline (*stiffly*) Oh? Awful, are they?
Barbara Absolutely! Wicked! (*To Robert*) The moment you go in one of them, you just want to leap on the bed!
Jacqueline Like a bordello?
Bernard Well, that's what bedrooms are for. (*Nudging Robert in the ribs*) What d'you say?
Robert (*with a frightened glance at Jacqueline*) You could say, er, yes, that bedrooms are ——
Barbara They certainly are. (*To Robert*) Why don't we do ours up in the same way?
Bernard You can't refuse your wife that now, can you?
Robert (*weakly*) I suppose not.
Bernard Why don't you go upstairs yourself and have a look. (*He winks at Robert*) You might get a few ideas.
Jacqueline No, no, we mustn't leave you on your own.
Bernard We'll be all right. Juliette and I are getting on like a house on fire. Aren't we, my dear? We'll have a glass of wine.
Barbara (*to Robert*) You should have a look, darling. The décor's rather spectacular.
Jacqueline Oh, I wouldn't say that. (*To Barbara; pointedly*) I mean, no mirrored ceilings or anything. (*To Robert*) But if you want to …

Act II, Scene 1							41

Robert tries to gesture that he does not want to go but Bernard bores in on him

Bernard Of course he does. And if they're going to do something similar, he'll have to.
Robert (*weakly*) Yes, I suppose that makes sense.
Jacqueline Right! (*Glaring at Robert; leading the way up the stairs*) Let's go then!

Robert follows Jacqueline upstairs

Bernard watches them exit and then moves to the drinks cabinet

Bernard I'm sorry, what was it you wanted again? Did we decide on Southern Comfort?
Barbara No, I've begun with champagne, so ...
Bernard You'll stick with it. Very wise. Did your husband explain why I asked you to come to dinner this evening?
Barbara He did. Something to do with stair rails? A contract, he said.
Bernard Yes, that's right. It's all about a contract.
Barbara He has to get you exactly what you want, he said.
Bernard Exactly! In fibreglass. Did he mention anything else to you?
Barbara No, I don't think so. Why? Was there something else he should have told me?
Bernard Well, perhaps not. Tell me, have you been married for long?
Barbara Er, no. Not too long. (*Hesitantly*) About five years.
Bernard You're much younger than him.
Barbara Yes, but I think it's good, that difference in our ages.
Bernard Really?
Barbara Yes. I prefer older men.
Bernard Do you? Why?
Barbara Let's say, it gives me a feeling of security, which I like to have.
Bernard And why's that?
Barbara Well, you see, the fact is — I'm his second wife.
Bernard Oh, really? I didn't know he'd been married before.
Barbara Yes. He has. I'm the second Madame Regnier.
Bernard Well, I must say, he's very lucky.
Barbara In what way?
Bernard Why, having you.
Barbara You're very complimentary.
Bernard Not at all. It's what I think. And I'm very lucky too.
Barbara Why?

Bernard Well, in meeting you this evening.
Barbara Now you're trying to make me blush again.
Bernard I don't see why I shouldn't say that.
Barbara If you want.
Bernard Especially since I find you quite enchanting company.
Barbara Really?
Bernard (*moving closer to her*) Oh, indeed.
Barbara Well, I'm not sure you're not being too —
Bernard Too what?
Barbara Let's say, er — too forward?
Bernard (*shrugging helplessly*) Too honest. What can I do? That's the way I am.
Barbara Maybe, but you're wasting your time.
Bernard Doing what?
Barbara Trying to hit on me. (*Adjusting quickly to a more prim attitude*) It may seem strange to you, but I'm an old-fashioned, faithful wife.

Barbara sits on the sofa and crosses her legs in a provocative way which suggest she is anything but

Bernard What? To Bobby?
Barbara Yes, of course to Bobby. Not all women cheat on their husbands, you know.

She crosses her legs in the other direction, equally provocatively

Bernard (*unable to take his eyes off her legs*) No, I'm sure. But most do, in my experience. And if a man doesn't know whether she will or not, he can at least try.
Barbara Do you try it on with all the women you meet?
Bernard No. Not at all.
Barbara Never?
Bernard No. In fact, I'll let you into a secret. I am faithful too.
Barbara Do you mean you've really never …
Bernard Never. That surprises you, doesn't it?
Barbara Yes. And no. (*Sadly*) Men always say that, don't they? (*She shrugs*) And then …
Bernard I've no reason to lie to you.
Barbara Then I'll believe you.
Bernard Good. That makes me very happy.
Barbara Why?
Bernard Because now, whatever we say, we can't play about, can we? Because we're both equally faithful.

Act II, Scene 1   43

For Barbara, this is sophistry. She shifts gear

Barbara Yes, that's right. But on the other hand, a lot of so-called faithful people aren't, are they?
Bernard Meaning?
Barbara I'm sure that for some, it's just because they've never had the opportunity.
Bernard You don't really believe that?
Barbara I'm certain of it.
Bernard It all depends. Let me give you an example. Something that happened quite recently. (*He pauses*) Well ...
Barbara Well? What?
Bernard I'm not sure I should tell you.
Barbara What difference does it make, one way or the other? Go on, tell me.
Bernard You really want to know?
Barbara Yes.
Bernard All right then. Do you remember when I opened the door for you?
Barbara Upstairs?
Bernard Yes. When we were together in the corridor. I brushed past you, to show you into the bedroom, and then ...

He sits next to her on the sofa. They look directly at each other

Barbara Yes?
Bernard I had a sudden overwhelming desire to ...

He moves in closer so they are face to face

Barbara To what?
Bernard (*making a joke of it*) To drag you down and roll over and over with you, right there on the bed!
Barbara (*equally lightly*) What? With your wife downstairs?
Bernard I completely forgot about her. And about Bobby. I couldn't think of anything or anyone but you. And then ...
Barbara Then?
Bernard (*sitting back*) Then, nothing.
Barbara Why?
Bernard Why? I wasn't going to make a pass and get my face slapped. Anyway, I pulled myself together.
Barbara That's a pity.
Bernard Pardon me?

Barbara Well, I may be a faithful wife but ...
Bernard Yes?
Barbara That may be because I've never wanted to be otherwise before. But I do have feelings sometimes.
Bernard You do? Or are you just teasing me, because of what I just told you?
Barbara No. I find you very attractive.

Barbara moves towards him. Bernard brushes his hand against her inviting lips

Bernard No, stop. I should never have said what I did. I'm sorry. (*Taking his hand away*) Do you really?
Barbara Yes.
Bernard Tell me more.
Barbara (*moving closer*) When I say I find you attractive, I mean ... distinguished looking. And you're kind of tough but you've got an air of class.
Bernard Really? You like that?
Barbara Yes. And you're fun to be with. Your eyes have a — a sparkle.
Bernard It's not that lamp, is it?
Barbara (*shaking her head*) No. It's something inside you that gives me a kind of tingle!
Bernard I'm beginning to feel funny too.

Barbara moves up right next to him and sighs deeply

Barbara Hold me!
Bernard (*holding her*) We shouldn't.

Barbara entwines herself around him

Barbara I want you.
Bernard We mustn't. (*He showers kisses on her*) Don't torture me.
Barbara Please.
Bernard No.
Barbara So it wasn't true, what you just told me?
Bernard Oh, yes, it was.
Barbara Then please!
Bernard We shouldn't. You know that.
Barbara I know. That's why it's so exciting.

She starts to pull him on top of her, on the sofa

Act II, Scene 1   45

Bernard They'll be coming back any moment now.
Barbara You're right. Let's make it quick. (*She starts to fumble with his fly*)

Marie-Louise enters from the kitchen. She does not see them at first

Marie-Louise By the way, I forgot —

She looks around the room, then starts as Barbara and Bernard both leap up from the couch, pulling rapidly apart

Bernard What the — Oh, it's you!
Marie-Louise (*looking around for someone else*) Yes.
Bernard You might have knocked.
Marie-Louise What, just to come in here?
Bernard Yes.

Marie-Louise watches as Barbara smoothes her ruffled clothing

Marie-Louise I've never been told that before.
Bernard (*defensively*) Well, you gave us a fright.
Marie-Louise I can see that.
Bernard Right then. What do you want?
Marie-Louise I came to ask Madame what she wants for dessert.
Bernard (*to Barbara*) What would you like?
Marie-Louise I didn't mean that madame.
Bernard There's no reason why our guest shouldn't choose. (*He turns to Barbara, blocking Marie-Louise's view*) What would you like?
Barbara (*in a stage whisper*) You!
Marie-Louise What?

Bernard coughs loudly to try and cover the confusion

Bernard (*to Barbara*) I'm not sure we have that.
Barbara I said *you*!
Bernard (*frantically*) Oh, ewe! Sheep! Lamb! Yes, baby lamb. What a good idea. (*To Marie-Louise*) Do we have any ewe?
Marie-Louise I thought we'd sorted out the main course.
Bernard Well, it doesn't matter. Serve whatever you like.
Marie-Louise Do you want heads or tails?
Bernard What? Serve whatever there is, every kind of dessert we've got.
Marie-Louise (*thoughtfully*) Mmm. (*Moving to the kitchen door*) That should make an interesting dish. A bit of rice pudding, a few grapes, a dash of yoghurt ...

Marie-Louise exits to the kitchen

Barbara immediately grabs hold of Bernard again, and starts to pull him towards the sofa

Barbara Come.
Bernard (*gesturing upstairs*) It's too late now.
Barbara If you don't, I shall tell them you sexually harassed me.
Bernard (*fondly*) You're mad.
Barbara For you.

They draw together for a long, deep kiss

Marie-Louise enters, interrupting them

Bernard What the — No! Not you again! I thought I told you to knock.
Marie-Louise What, to come in here?
Bernard I've already said so.
Marie-Louise I thought you were having me on.
Bernard All right, what d'you want this time?
Marie-Louise I've got a problem. I need to ask Madame something.
Bernard No.
Marie-Louise No? You don't want cheese before the dessert then?
Bernard No!
Marie-Louise No. Right. Fine. It's a bit over-ripe anyway. (*As she goes*) At least there won't be any smell.

Marie-Louise exits to the kitchen

Barbara advances on Bernard again. He retreats until his back is against the study door. Just as Barbara winds herself round him again, we hear Jacqueline's (false) laugh

Jacqueline comes down the stairs, followed by Robert

Bernard immediately breaks away to greet them

Bernard Well, what d'you think, Bobby?
Robert Excellent. Very well designed.
Bernard It is, isn't it? I think all bedrooms should be …
Barbara Inspiring.
Bernard (*to Barbara*) The very word.

Act II, Scene 1

Marie-Louise enters

Marie-Louise Tell me again what you asked for.
Jacqueline What?
Marie-Louise Oh, you're here. Good. About the wines, do you want white or red?
Jacqueline Both.
Marie-Louise In what order?
Jacqueline (*shortly*) You should know what order. White with the fish and red to follow. And as it's such a pleasant evening, we'll dine on the terrace.
Robert That's a very good idea.
Marie-Louise (*sniffily*) It may be for you lot. It doesn't make my task any easier.

Marie-Louise sweeps off back to the kitchen

Jacqueline Let's go and finish our drinks while we're waiting, shall we?
Robert That's a good idea too.
Bernard You go out. I'll fetch them for you.
Jacqueline Right. (*To Barbara*) After you.

With a reluctant glance back at Bernard, Barbara exits to the terrace. Jacqueline follows. They move out of sight

Robert holds back, then checks the others have gone out before

Robert (*to Bernard; hissing*) Well?
Bernard What?
Robert How did you get on with Juliette?
Bernard She's quite charming. Surprisingly receptive.
Robert Then you struck lucky. (*Nodding towards the terrace*) You'd better get a move on.
Bernard I have to be a bit cautious. You did say she's always been faithful to you.
Robert She has. But you know what some women are like. They're faithful just because they've never had the chance to be otherwise.
Bernard (*after a pause*) Do you know, someone else told me that.
Robert It's well known. So, like I told you, make your move now. It all depends on you.
Bernard It's easy to say that.
Robert If you want her, you've got to go for it. She'll resist, of course, but don't be put off. Force her!

Bernard This is a change of attitude, isn't it?
Robert It'll upset me, of course. I'm not saying I like the idea. I'll be heartbroken but, well, if it's a choice between that and having my body broken ... (*Shrugging; desolately*) What good would I be to her then?
Bernard That's very touching.

The doorbell rings

Robert I love her, I want to grow old with her. That's why I'm depending on you.
Bernard (*patting Robert's arm sympathetically*) I understand your logic. And I'll do my best.
Robert Thank you. This is really very difficult for me, you know. I shall be devastated after this. I don't know what I'll do.
Bernard There isn't anything to do, yet. But I'll keep you informed.

Marie-Louise enters

Marie-Louise Did you ring?
Bernard No. There's someone at the door. But I'm not expecting anyone. Send them away.
Marie-Louise (*wiping her hands on her apron*) There's always a warm welcome at this house.
Bernard (*ignoring her*) Let's finish our drinks outside. They'll be wondering what we're conspiring about.
Robert I must say, a bit of fresh air wouldn't go amiss.

Bernard and Robert go on to the terrace and out of sight

Marie-Louise goes to answer the front door

Marie-Louise (*off; politely*) Hello.

Marie-Louise and Juliette enter the living-room. Juliette wears a rather drab suit with a bolero jacket and carries a handbag. Her hair is tied up in a bun

Juliette Thank you.
Marie-Louise Can I help you?
Juliette I am expected.
Marie-Louise Not by me.
Juliette Perhaps they forgot to tell you.
Marie-Louise Well, that wouldn't surprise me.

Act II, Scene 1

Juliette I was invited to dine here.
Marie-Louise Now that does surprise me.
Juliette Why?
Marie-Louise Because I was told to lay for four, and with you it would make five.
Juliette If there are already four present, you were probably told to lay for six.
Marie-Louise Why? Are there two of you?
Juliette There ought to be but my husband couldn't make it. So I came alone.
Marie-Louise (*at the end of her tether*) So, you're going to be five? Not four, as I was told. And not six. Just five!
Juliette Would you repeat that?
Marie-Louise Never mind. Don't worry about it. It's only me who's put out. I suppose I'd better go and tell them you've arrived.
Juliette Thank you.

In a bad temper, Marie-Louise stumps off towards the terrace, then pauses and glances back at Juliette

Marie-Louise What name shall I say?
Juliette Madame Regnier. Juliette Regnier.
Marie-Louise Regnier.

Marie-Louise continues to the terrace, then halts as if she's been stabbed in the back. She turns to Juliette

   You did say Regnier?
Juliette Correct.

Marie-Louise shrugs helplessly and starts back towards the terrace

   Bernard enters from the terrace, closing the glass doors behind him

Bernard Is everything all right?
Marie-Louise You tell me. (*In a harsh whisper*) There's someone here pretending to be somebody else.
Bernard (*frowning; puzzled*) Really? (*To Juliette*) Good-evening, madame.
Juliette Good-evening.

Bernard notices Marie-Louise is still hanging around

Bernard (*to Marie-Louise*) Take some ice and champagne on to the terrace. (*He opens the terrace door for Mary-Louise*)
Marie-Louise I don't see why. It's what they've already got out there.

Bernard opens the terrace door. Marie-Louise exits to the terrace with the champagne and ice

Bernard (*to Juliette; smiling*) What can I do for you, madame?
Juliette Are you perhaps Monsieur Marcellin?
Bernard Indeed I am.
Juliette I'm delighted to make your acquaintance.

She holds out her hand. Bernard takes it politely

   I am Madame Regnier.

Bernard drops her hand as if it were a lighted coal

Bernard I beg your pardon?
Juliette I am Juliette Regnier. You invited me here.
Bernard (*struggling to understand*) You mean you're Bobby's — I mean, Robert's wife?
Juliette Yes, I am.
Bernard (*dawning on him*) Bastard!
Juliette I beg your pardon!?
Bernard (*quickly recovering*) I said, the bar's there — bar's there — if you'd like a drink … (*Unsure how to play this*) I'm sorry, I, er …
Juliette I understand. You're surprised to see me on my own?
Bernard Er, yes, in a manner of speaking.
Juliette It's because my husband couldn't come.
Bernard He couldn't?
Juliette I'm afraid not. When I received your invitation, he'd already rung me to say that he would be out for the whole evening. And he'd left his mobile at home, of course.
Bernard Of course. I see. The whole evening?
Juliette And so, since he wasn't aware of your invitation, it wasn't possible for him to make his apologies.
Bernard Ah, I see. Now I'm beginning to understand.
Juliette I tried to call you but you are ex-directory, it seems.
Bernard That's perfectly true. I am sorry.
Juliette So I thought I'd better come, anyway, to explain why you hadn't heard from him.
Bernard I'm very glad you did. It was most thoughtful of you.

Act II, Scene 1   51

Juliette I'm sure he would have loved to accept, but he works so hard all the time.
Bernard (*nodding sympathetically*) Long hours?
Juliette Oh lord, yes. He has meetings all the time. Often unexpected and always at the last moment — even on Saturdays!
Bernard (*feigning astonishment*) No! Not Saturdays!
Juliette Yes, as you can see.
Bernard Yes, I do see. Very clearly now. Are you sure I can't offer you something to drink?
Juliette Thank you, but I don't drink.
Bernard Then do sit down. Please.

Juliette perches on the edge of the chair

Juliette Thank you.
Bernard No, properly.

He gives her a little prod and she falls back in the chair

I don't want you to fall off.
Juliette Why should I do that?
Bernard I mean, when I tell you your husband is here.
Juliette (*delighted*) Oh I see. It was here that he was having his meeting this evening. And he didn't know we'd been invited for dinner. What a coincidence!
Bernard Well, I don't think you'd quite call it a coincidence.
Juliette No?
Bernard No. You see, the reason he is here is because he's my wife's lover.
Juliette What?
Bernard Now you see why I wanted you to sit down.
Juliette That's just not possible. I don't believe you.
Bernard As you wish. But you'd be wrong.
Juliette I have a perfect husband. He's not in the least interested in sex — I mean, outside the home, of course.
Bernard You think so? I believed exactly the same about my wife.
Juliette She can do what she likes, it doesn't concern me.
Bernard I'm afraid it does. You see, it's with my wife that your husband spends his Saturdays.
Juliette You don't know what you're talking about. My Robert is always busy working.
Bernard I assure you, your dear Robert still finds time to put himself about. With my wife.

Juliette (*with scornful disbelief*) And you accept that?
Bernard No I don't. I was presented with a *fait accompli*. Which I now present to you.
Juliette I want to see my husband! Immediately!
Bernard And do you think he's going to admit what I've just told you?
Juliette No. He won't admit it. Because your story is absurd!
Bernard He won't admit it because he is a liar. But if you want proof …
Juliette Oh, yes, I do. Since you're making such outrageous accusations, I definitely do.
Bernard Very well. You'll have it. Let's see. (*Looking around*) Oh, yes. Right. Get yourself behind there.

Bernard leads Juliette to the curtain which hang by the terrace doors

Juliette What for?
Bernard I'm going to find an excuse to get my wife and your husband together, in here. I'd be amazed if they don't give themselves away.

Before Juliette can protest, he calls out to the terrace

(*Calling to Jacqueline*) Darling, could you come here a second?
Jacqueline (*off*) Yes, I'm coming.

Juliette hastily conceals herself behind the curtain

Bernard (*to Juliette; hissing*) Don't move!

Juliette pops her head round from the curtain

Juliette Well I'm not a complete idiot!

Juliette disappears again as Jacqueline enters from the terrace

Jacqueline What is it?
Bernard Marie-Louise can't get the ice cubes out so I said I'd give her a hand. (*Moving towards the kitchen door*) Would you stay in here? I left a message for someone to call me. If it comes through while I'm in the kitchen, just give me a shout.
Jacqueline Will you be long?
Bernard No, just a few minutes. Give Bobby another drink.

Bernard exits through the kitchen door

Act II, Scene 1   53

Jacqueline moves back towards the terrace

Jacqueline (*calling out to her guests*) Can I get you something?
Barbara (*off*) I'm OK, thanks.
Robert (*off*) Yes, please. Dying for one.

Jacqueline moves to the drinks cabinet

Robert comes in from the terrace

Jacqueline Whisky, I suppose?
Robert Thank you.

Jacqueline pours him a drink and hands it to him

D'you know, I think it's all working out rather well.
Jacqueline For you perhaps.

Jacqueline and Robert have their backs to the terrace doors. Juliette's head pops out from behind the curtain. Throughout the following Juliette's head appears and disappears from behind the curtain

Robert No, for both of us. He doesn't suspect a thing.
Jacqueline Oh, right. Great. Except it's me who's being cheated on.
Robert Well, no more than my wife.

Juliette screws up her nose

She doesn't make a fuss about it.

Juliette's mouth drops open

Jacqueline She doesn't know about it.
Robert Thank God for that.

Juliette is suddenly seized by a desire to sneeze. She opens her mouth wide to try and suppress it but cannot. She muffles it by putting her head behind the curtain

Jacqueline Bless you.
Robert What?
Jacqueline I said, bless you.
Robert Why?

Jacqueline Because you sneezed.
Robert I thought it was you.
Jacqueline No, it wasn't me.
Robert Then who was it?
Jacqueline (*gesturing towards the terrace*) It must have been her.
Robert Oh, damn. This is no time for her to catch a cold, I want her to get on with the job.

Robert takes Jacqueline in his arms

Darling! You do love me, don't you?
Jacqueline You know I do.

Robert and Jacqueline kiss. Juliette sneezes again. Robert disengages himself

Robert That's it! I'm going to tell her to wrap up!
Jacqueline But that sneeze didn't come from the terrace. It came from inside, not out.

Juliette, unseen by them, makes desperate efforts not to sneeze again. She holds a finger under her nose

Robert Well, how could it have been? (*He mounts a few stairs and looks up, then comes down again*) There's no one here. (*He takes a good look around*) You can see for yourself. We're alone.

Robert moves towards the terrace again and Jacqueline starts to follow him

Bernard enters from the kitchen with an ice bucket and a bottle of champagne

Juliette gives an enormous sneeze. Bernard freezes. Jacqueline and Robert stop in their tracks and turn to see Bernard

Jacqueline Gesundheit.
Bernard Thanks.

Bernard sniffs and wipes a finger under his nose

Robert Oh, it was you who was sneezing?

Bernard can see that Juliette is going to sneeze again

Act II, Scene 1   55

Bernard I'm afraid so.

Bernard sneezes in synch with Juliette

Robert Oh, dear. You were right. It wasn't coming from the terrace.
Bernard No, that's right. It was me. In there. (*Indicating the kitchen door*) You get a sort of echo. It's the concrete, it reflects the sound. Sort of boomerangs off. (*Demonstrating*) Hah!
Juliette Hah!
Robert (*blinking*) I see.
Bernard (*to Jacqueline*) Any calls?
Jacqueline Not so far.
Bernard I'd better ring myself.

He takes a lump of ice from the bucket and drops it in Robert's glass, then hands the bucket to Jacqueline

Here. And don't let that poor girl die of thirst out there.
Robert No, no, of course not.

Robert follows Jacqueline back out to the terrace and out of sight

Bernard (*to Juliette*) Are you all right?
Juliette (*emerging from behind the curtain*) No, I feel terrible. (*She muffles another sneeze*) The dust in those curtains! Why don't you get them cleaned?
Bernard My wife's been busy, doing other things. Well?
Juliette Give me a whisky, would you? A large one.
Bernard I thought you didn't drink?
Juliette I do now.
Bernard You're convinced then?

Bernard pours a large drink and hands it to her

Juliette It's disgraceful. (*She downs the Scotch in one gulp*) To treat me like that!
Bernard And me.
Juliette I don't give a bugger about you.
Bernard Thanks a lot.
Juliette I mean to say, you knew. I didn't.
Bernard Well, yes. (*Sympathetically*) It must have been a shock.
Juliette Huh! A shock? I feel as though I want to scream! In fact, I think I will.

Juliette opens her mouth to scream. Bernard quickly pacifies her

Bernard No, no. Stay calm. Sit down.
Juliette Sit? The way I feel? You're not serious?
Bernard Look, I'm sorry if I've upset you but let me try and cheer you up.
Juliette It's useless.
Bernard On the contrary, it's essential. Because you don't know what happens next.
Juliette What happens next?
Bernard Sit down and have your drink. (*She hands him her empty glass*) Have another drink.

Juliette sits as Bernard goes to the drinks cabinet, refills the glass and hands it to her. Juliette knocks it straight back

Juliette Thank you. (*She hiccoughs slightly*) I'm listening.
Bernard Right. When I found out that my wife was deceiving me with your husband, I told him — either I pay someone to have you killed, or you sleep with me.
Juliette Bobby's not like that.
Bernard No. You. With me.
Juliette But you're mad. I wouldn't dream of doing such a thing.
Bernard Exactly. And that's why he's brought someone more amenable as a replacement.
Juliette (*ironically*) To protect my honour? How very delicate.
Bernard How very tricky! Knowing that he couldn't count on your participation, he prefers to bring a substitute. A most attractive stand-in, I admit. But your husband isn't going to make a fool of me. The boot's on the other foot.
Juliette Good. I'd like to see that.
Bernard You shall. I'll show you. Now, what shall we call you?
Juliette You know who I am. Juliette Regnier.
Bernard No, that's the name of your stand-in.
Juliette (*shaking her head*) I'm out of my depth.
Bernard OK, let's say you're ... Pepita Goussard.
Juliette Who? Why?
Bernard Because the phoney Juliette Regnier is already out there on the terrace and it wouldn't do to have two of them.
Juliette No, it wouldn't. So I have to be Pepita Goussard? (*Clutching her head*) I'm going to have a nervous breakdown!
Bernard It's no bother to me if you prefer to be called something else. How about Blanche Levy?

Act II, Scene 1   57

Juliette There must be an alternative to Blanche Levy!
Bernard Would you prefer Nicole?
Juliette I was talking about Levy!
Bernard Well you can pronounce it differently. How about Levée? L-e-v-é-e.
Juliette Ah, like that. Yes, that's better. All right, let's settle on Nicole Levée.
Bernard Good. Now listen — I'll show you. (*Calling towards the terrace*) Madame Regnier? Juliette?
Barbara (*off*) Coming.
Bernard You see? When I call you, she answers.
Juliette I'm going to give him such hell about this.
Bernard Just watch what happens next.

Barbara enters from the terrace. She smiles at Juliette

Barbara You called me?
Bernard Yes, I'd like you to meet a friend of mine who just called in to say hello. Because, when I mentioned your name to her, she said, "How extraordinary. I know Juliette Regnier very well." (*To Juliette*) Didn't you?
Juliette Yes, that's right. I did.
Barbara (*not knowing what to do; embarrassed*) Really?
Juliette And you're not Juliette Regnier!
Barbara (*trying to bluff it out*) How d'you mean, I'm not?
Juliette Because you're not. And if you want to know how I know, it's because I ——
Bernard (*stepping between the two of them*) Ts, ts, ts, ts.
Barbara What?
Bernard Nicole was trying to say that ... (*Indicating Juliette*) Sorry, this is Nicole.
Juliette Nicole Levée. L-e-v-é-e.
Bernard You don't know that name?
Barbara (*all at sea*) Well, er, um ...
Bernard Then obviously it's a different Juliette Regnier that Nicole knows.
Juliette Yes. Amazing coincidence, isn't it? She's a close friend, a very dear friend who ——
Bernard Shh!
Juliette What?
Bernard We've solved the mystery. There must be another Juliette Regnier, that's all. (*To Juliette*) Do you see?
Juliette (*reluctantly*) I see.

Bernard (*to Barbara*) So, now you know there are two Juliette Regniers. There may even be others. Who knows?
Barbara Well, I'm sorry.
Juliette No more than I am.
Bernard That's right. Nicole's sorry not to see her friend. Aren't you, Nicole?
Juliette Shattered!
Barbara (*uneasily*) Oh well, I must be getting back to, er ... (*She holds out a hand*) Good-night.

Barbara and Juliette shake hands

Juliette Good-night

Barbara moves towards the terrace

(*To Barbara; loudly*) Juliette! Regnier!

Barbara forces a smile, waves a hand, then closes the glass doors behind her as she exits to the terrace

What a nerve! What a damned nerve! I'd a good mind to set about her!
Bernard Then it's lucky you didn't. The game's not over yet.
Juliette If my husband had been in here, she wouldn't have dared pass herself off like that!
Bernard You think not?
Juliette Absolutely not! And I want to see him right now!
Bernard But then he'd realize immediately that I know the other Juliette is an impostor!
Juliette What about it?
Bernard Well, since you have no desire to sacrifice yourself to me, it's Bobby who's got to be made to pay. Think about it. If I call your husband in here, you'll blow his cover, put an end to the game. However, if you really want to see him, that could still be arranged.
Juliette How?
Bernard In the same way that we just dealt with the impostor.
Juliette (*owlishly*) How is that?
Bernard Well, it's difficult. But not impossible.
Juliette What's not?
Bernard All it needs is for you to continue to be Nicole Levée.
Juliette (*ridiculing the idea*) He'd never believe that!
Bernard Why not?
Juliette Because he'll recognize me!

Act II, Scene 1   59

Bernard Of course he will. Which is why he won't be able to say anything. All you've got to do is stick it out. Believe it yourself!
Juliette He'll recognize my jewellery.
Bernard Give it to me.
Juliette (*removing her rings*) Don't lose them. This one's a diamond solitaire he gave me.
Bernard Bobby's very generous.
Juliette With my father's money, he is.
Bernard I see. He gives you the jewels but he doesn't buy them.
Juliette Wedding ring too?
Bernard Definitely. Most important, for this occasion.
Juliette (*handing Bernard her wedding ring*) The pearl earrings are not real.
Bernard Even so, we don't want to draw attention to them.

Juliette takes off her earrings and hands them to Bernard, who puts them in his pocket with the other jewellery

Juliette What about my clothes?
Bernard You can keep them on. That's a nothing style, anyway.
Juliette That's true. And anyway, he's never seen it. It's new.
Bernard That's good. Let your hair down.
Juliette You really think this will work?
Bernard Absolutely. It's Bobby who's going to have the problem.
Juliette How're we going to do this exactly?
Bernard Well, you're going out.
Juliette Now?
Bernard Yes, out there. (*He points to the hallway*) And then you'll hear ... (*Levelling a finger at her*) Pouf, pouf!
Juliette Are you going to shoot him?
Bernard No. But when you hear "pouf, pouf" you can ring the bell.
Juliette Why?
Bernard It's just a secret signal between us, that's all. For you to ring.

He goes out to the front door

(*Off*) Like this.

He rings the doorbell twice

(*Off*) You see?
Juliette (*addressing the hallway*) That's easy enough. You are going to say "pouf, pouf"?
Bernard (*off*) Correct. And then you ring the bell.

Bernard comes to the hall doorway

We'll leave the door open so you can hear.

Juliette goes out to the front door

Bernard comes back into the living-room

Marie-Louise enters

Marie-Louise What now?
Bernard What do you want?
Marie-Louise Me? Nothing. But if I have to keep leaving the kitchen, dinner will never be ready.
Bernard Then you'd better stay in there.
Marie-Louise What?
Bernard I said, don't leave the kitchen.
Marie-Louise But someone rang the bell.
Bernard Yes, I did.
Marie-Louise No, I mean someone outside.
Bernard That's right. I told you, it was me.
Marie-Louise You went out and rang the bell?
Bernard Yes.
Marie-Louise Why?
Bernard Why not? To amuse myself!
Marie-Louise It amuses you to ring a bell?
Bernard I just told you.
Marie-Louise You've got nothing better to do than ring a doorbell?
Bernard No.
Marie-Louise (*after a pause*) Well, if that's what turns you on, I don't mind.
Bernard It's just a bit of fun, that's all. So if you hear the bell, you won't need to answer it.
Marie-Louise It'll be you ringing?
Bernard Well, perhaps not me.
Marie-Louise I see. (*She doesn't see*) Someone else gets a kick out of bell ringing too, is that it?
Bernard Yes, that's it.
Marie-Louise Your wife?
Bernard No.
Marie-Louise Ah. (*Indicating the terrace with her thumb*) One of the guests out there.
Bernard No. Someone else.

Act II, Scene 1   61

Marie-Louise (*after a pause*) Who's going to ring?
Bernard Correct.
Marie-Louise (*trying to understand; slowly*) So you know someone's going to ring the doorbell?
Bernard Yes.
Marie-Louise But it might not be who you expect. It could be anyone.
Bernard Look, you just don't understand.
Marie-Louise You can say that again. I don't. But just suppose this person doesn't come?

Bernard gestures impatience

Would you like me to ring the doorbell for you?
Bernard No, I would not. That would be useless.
Marie-Louise All right, be like that! (*She moves towards the kitchen door, then pauses*) I suppose, if the worst came to the worst, you could always ring it yourself.
Bernard Well there you go. So there's no need for you to worry about it.

Bernard takes Marie-Louise's arm and escorts her towards the kitchen door

Marie-Louise OK, OK. If it rings, I'll know it's ringing, but it won't really be ringing. Not properly.
Bernard That's it.
Marie-Louise Fair enough. Suits me. Enjoy your bell ringing.

Marie-Louise returns to the kitchen

Robert comes in from the terrace

Robert Juliette asked me to come and find you.
Bernard Your wife?
Robert Yes. She wants to see you. It proves you interest her, anyway.
Bernard She likes me then?
Robert I'm sure she does.
Bernard Well, that's lucky for you my friend, because if she didn't ... (*He points a finger threateningly*) Pouf, pouf!
Robert Pouf, pouf?
Bernard Maybe. I don't know yet what the hit men will decide. It might be the truck — boom!

Robert flinches

Or with a gun. (*Pointing his finger again; louder*) Pouf, pouf!

The doorbell rings

Robert (*nervously*) But it's all set. You know that. Believe me, it'll all work out fine.
Bernard I'm telling you for the last time, it'd better! Otherwise — pouf, pouf!

The doorbell rings again. Bernard moves towards the hallway

Robert (*desperately*) But you'll get what you want. It's up to you.
Bernard No, no, my friend. It's up to your wife!

Bernard exits to the front door

Robert turns away in despair

(*Off; to Juliette*) Good-evening.

Bernard and Juliette enter the living-room

Juliette How are you?
Bernard How are you? This is a surprise!
Juliette I was just passing, thought I'd look in.
Bernard It's lovely to see you. Let me introduce you to Robert Regnier.

The previously distracted Robert turns to see Juliette, then promptly turns away again and starts to sidle back towards the terrace. Bernard halts him

The Lights fade to Black-out

Scene 2

The same. Immediately following

Bernard Robert, I'd like you to meet a friend of mine, Nicole Levy.
Juliette Levée. V-é-e.
Robert (*without turning; in a strangulated voice*) Good-evening.

Act II, Scene 2   63

Robert tries again to reach the sanctuary of the terrace

Bernard No, don't go nipping off, old chap. Come on.

Robert decides the only escape is to have a fit. He covers his face with his hands, coughing and grunting as though about to choke, while jerking his body violently, all the time still trying to get away

Juliette What's wrong with him?
Bernard I don't know. I've never seen him like that, (*To Robert; concerned*) What is it? Are you all right?

Robert, forced to turn back towards Bernard, remains doubled up, groaning pathetically. For extra protection, he covers his face with his hand, as if he had toothache or something. He tries again to get away but Bernard insists on blocking him

He doesn't seem to be very well, does he?
Juliette Either that or he's had a shock of some sort.
Robert No, no, ooer, um, aaah, no shock, no — ugh!

Robert's string of babble is designed to put them at their ease and let him go, but Bernard refuses, still blocking him

Juliette If it's not that, what is it?
Bernard I can't make it out. (*To Robert*) What is it, old chap? Won't you tell me?

Robert turns his face to the wall which he grips as though he'd like to climb it, at the same time still hopping and coughing, all punctuated with inarticulate moans

Robert Oooh, oooh, aaah.
Bernard Look, Bobby, you must try and pull yourself together.
Robert Ugh! Can't! Must go. Aah.
Bernard You can't? Can't what?
Juliette Can't face it?
Bernard I can't make out what's happened to him. It's almost as if you somehow gave him a fright.
Juliette Well I can't see why that should be.
Bernard No.

Robert lets out another pathetic moan. He also tries to make another move towards the terrace but Bernard won't let him

We can't help you if you won't tell us what's wrong.

Bernard taps Robert sharply on the head

Robert Oh!
Bernard Have you got a headache?

Robert protects his head. Bernard digs him in the stomach

Robert Ow!
Bernard Or is it your tummy? Listen, you might at least say hello to Nicole. She's having dinner with us.

Robert promptly has another fit, all the time keeping his face turned away, moaning and groaning

Robert No, no ... not Nicole ... no dinner — Oooh!
Bernard (*strictly*) Robert, I do wish you'd tell me what your problem is. And where. (*Prodding Robert*) Is it here? Here?

Bernard sharply prods Robert all over his body: in the chest, arms, legs, backside even. Robert cries out with each jab, leaping finally as though he'd been goosed. In between he continues to cough and groan. As Bernard tries to turn him to face Juliette, Robert decides the time has come to black-out altogether. He falls into Bernard's arms. Juliette gives a little cry

Juliette Aah! He's fainted!
Bernard So he has! Give me hand. I'll go and get a damp cloth.

They lift him and stretch him out on the sofa, where he lies gasping

Bernard shrugs to Juliette as if to say " Well, what did I tell you?" and then goes off into the kitchen

Juliette remains with Robert. She leans over him

Juliette Come along now, monsieur.

Robert opens a single eye and sees Juliette. Then he open the other eye, takes a look around, and sees they are alone. He sits up with a jerk, as though spring-loaded

Act II, Scene 2

Robert What the hell are you doing here?
Juliette Well that's very polite, I must say.
Robert Cut it out. Stop playing the fool.
Juliette I'm not going to take this.
Robert Listen, you can't stay here!
Juliette But I've only just arrived.
Robert You must go! Or it's the truck!
Juliette What truck?
Robert You mustn't let him find out!
Juliette The truck driver?
Robert No, him! Bernard! That man's a gangster!
Juliette Oh, is he? What mustn't he find out?
Robert That you're my wife.
Juliette I think you must be delirious.
Robert You can't fool me, Juliette.
Juliette Nicole. My name is Nicole.
Robert Look, stop this pantomime! It's me.
Juliette Yes, you are you. Nobody disputes that.
Robert (*struggling to his feet*) That's enough! Can we have done with this stupid game?
Juliette I'm warning you, if you don't stop insulting me, you'll have my husband to deal with.
Robert But you're my husband!
Juliette Now you have gone mad!
Robert I mean, I'm your husband!
Juliette This is all your imagination.
Robert (*angrily*) Stop buggering about! I know you're my wife!
Juliette You've got an obsession about this.

Robert, confused, begins to retreat, doubting his own mind

Robert Have I? But it couldn't be! No, it's just not possible, that you're her exact double ...
Juliette Whose double?
Robert Your own.
Juliette I think you mean your wife's, don't you? Perhaps we bear a superficial resemblance?
Robert No, no!
Juliette Well, if we are lookalikes, I'm sure she'll be delighted to know.
Robert (*still unable to believe it*) It's not true — it can't be. Can it? Or am I going completely mad?
Juliette Well, you do give that impression.

Bernard enters from the kitchen with a damp cloth

Bernard Is he any better?

On seeing Bernard, Robert whirls round and collapses on to the couch. He lets out an agonized sigh, like a wounded animal. Juliette signals to Bernard that, nevertheless, Robert is still taking everything in

Juliette No, I don't think he is. Would you believe it — he's convinced that I am his wife?
Bernard No! How ridiculous. You don't look in the least like his wife. (*He slaps Robert's face to and fro with the damp cloth*) What on earth's got into you?
Robert Ow! Ow!
Bernard Nicole is already married. (*He slaps Robert with the cloth*)
Robert Ow! Ow!
Bernard Your wife is on the terrace. Her name is Juliette. (*He slaps Robert with the cloth again*) Remember?
Robert Ow! No. Ow! Yes.
Bernard Look, pull yourself together, mate! (*Calling; to the terrace*) Juliette!
Juliette Yes?
Bernard No, I'm calling his wife.
Juliette Well, he keeps calling me his wife!
Bernard I know. But you're Nicole, and she's Juliette.
Juliette He's driving me mad now.
Bernard (*calling; to the terrace*) Juliette! She'd better take a look at him. Perhaps she's used to dealing with these crises?

Barbara and Jacqueline come in from the terrace, concerned

Jacqueline What's happening?
Bernard Bobby's been taken ill. (*To Barbara*) Has this happened before?
Barbara (*hurrying to Robert's side*) No, I've never seen him like this.

Juliette's face is a picture as Barbara gently smoothes Robert's brow

Robert Ooh! Oooh!
Jacqueline I'm going to call a doctor.

Jacqueline moves towards the telephone. Bernard stops her

Act II, Scene 2   67

Bernard No, I think he's coming round a bit. Perhaps a bit of fresh air will do him good.
Robert (*anything to get out of this*) Mm. Mmm.
Barbara I think you're right. (*To Robert*) Come on, my precious.

Juliette looks as though she will burst as Barbara slips her arm under Robert's shoulders and helps him to his feet. He keeps his eyes closed

Robert (*feigning pain*) Oooh!
Barbara (*gently*) Come on now.

As Robert staggers, Barbara slaps his face

What's wrong with you? (*Slapping him harder*) You mustn't let yourself get into this state.
Robert (*brought out of it by Barbara*) I'm sick!
Barbara Have you got a pain? Does it hurt? (*Cooing*) Tell pussykins where it hurts.

Unseen by Jacqueline, Bernard and Juliette exchange glances

Barbara begins to assist the limping Robert towards the terrace

Robert (*gasping*) Nowhere — everywhere.
Jacqueline He's acting really strangely.
Juliette Imagining things. He was going on about some truck.
Bernard (*indicating Juliette*) Yes, it seemed to hit him when he saw ...

Jacqueline stares at Juliette. Bernard remembers they have not been introduced

I don't think you know each other. My wife — Nicole Levée. V-é-e.
Jacqueline (*frowning; puzzled*) How do you do.

Juliette watches Barbara escort Robert out on to the terrace and out of sight

Juliette How do you do.
Bernard I'm involved in some business with Nicole's husband. Levée. Have I mentioned Levée?
Jacqueline No.
Bernard Yes, I'm sure I did. You just don't remember.
Jacqueline Obviously not. Anyway, what was that all about?

Bernard He just went, just like that, as soon as he saw Nicole. I'd better go and see what he's up to. I'll be right back.

Bernard exits to the terrace and out of sight

Jacqueline (*to Juliette*) Funny, I've got the feeling I know you from somewhere ...
Juliette Really?
Jacqueline Yes, I'm sure we've met. I've certainly seen you before.
Juliette Perhaps in the street, out shopping?
Jacqueline Could be.
Juliette Or maybe you're confusing me with someone else, like that poor gentleman. What was his name?
Jacqueline Regnier?
Juliette Yes, that's it. Monsieur Regnier. When he was delirious, he seemed to think I was someone he knew.
Jacqueline (*looking hard at Juliette*) I'm still sure that we've met.

Bernard enters from the terrace

Bernard He seems to have calmed down a bit now, thank heavens. (*To Juliette*) I really can't apologize enough for all this.

Bernard gestures out to the terrace. Juliette shrugs in return

Juliette Oh, these things happen.
Bernard I know! (*Moving to the drinks cabinet*) We'll give him another snifter. That'll help him get himself together.
Jacqueline (*to Juliette; politely*) Yes, sorry about all this. But I do hope you'll be able to stop for dinner.
Juliette (*gesturing thanks*) I'm afraid I'm going on somewhere.
Bernard Well, give them a ring, tell them you'll be there later. (*To Jacqueline*) You don't mind too much about all this, do you, darling? He should be coming round by now. Poor old Bobby.

Bernard rings the service bell

Jacqueline I'll go and see. (*To Juliette*) Come and have some champagne on the terrace. (*Moving* US) D'you know, the more I look at you, the more I'm convinced I've seen you somewhere before. It'll come to me soon, for sure.
Juliette I don't think so, but perhaps you have.

Jacqueline and Juliette go out on to the terrace

Act II, Scene 2

Marie-Louise enters from the kitchen

Marie-Louise Did you ring?
Bernard Yes.
Marie-Louise For fun? Or did you want me?
Bernard Just to tell you to lay another place.
Marie-Louise Making five?
Bernard Correct.
Marie-Louise I was told to prepare for four, which is five including me. I have to eat as well, you know. So if I lay an extra place I have to prepare for six.
Bernard Whatever! What's the problem?
Marie-Louise Well, the way it stands at present, I've only prepared for five.
Bernard And what prevents you from making it six.
Marie-Louise Nothing, so long as I've got enough in the freezer!
Bernard It may be that one of us won't be eating.
Marie-Louise Probably me!
Bernard No, Monsieur Regnier. He's got an upset stomach.
Marie-Louise Right, so there'll only be four of you?
Bernard Probably. But there might be five.
Marie-Louise Oh well, I'll just have to work it out, won't I? As usual!

Barbara enters from the terrace

Marie-Louise stares at Barbara. Barbara stares back. Bernard looks at both of them and they look at him

Bernard (*to Marie-Louise*) Well? What are you waiting for?
Marie-Louise Me? Nothing, I was just trying to work out who's who. (*Staring at Barbara*) This is going to be a very peculiar dinner. (*As she stumps to the kitchen door*) Very!

Marie-Lousie exits

Bernard So how is he?
Barbara Well, he was getting better. But the moment Nicole Levée came on the terrace, he started again, you know, writhing and moaning.
Bernard Very odd.
Barbara I've never seen him in such a state.
Bernard I shouldn't bother about him any more.
Barbara What?
Bernard Well, you're not his wife. Why should you?
Barbara Oh! You know!

Bernard Yes, I know. But he doesn't know I know.
Barbara That makes me feel awful!
Bernard Why?
Barbara (*producing a cheque from her cleavage*) He gave me a cheque for a thousand euros.
Bernard That doesn't seem a lot for a girl like you, to sleep with someone you don't even know.
Barbara That was only half.
Bernard Only half? Well, a girl has to live, I suppose. Or perhaps you do it to pay the rest home bills for your poor old mother?
Barbara I don't have a poor old mother.
Bernard So you just do it for the money?
Barbara No. Not just that.
Bernard Why then?
Barbara I like life to be a bit of adventure. Fun. And the way he put it to me, this was like a bet, a sort of joke.
Bernard And you took it on? For a bet, like a joke?
Barbara (*shrugging*) I said I'd come to dinner, that's all. I didn't guarantee anything else.
Bernard All the same.
Barbara So ... (*She tears up the cheque in front of him, very deliberately*)
Bernard You didn't need to do that. Come on!
Barbara No. If I don't deliver, then it's no deal.
Bernard But you could say you did?
Barbara I'm not like that. It so happens I was attracted to you, I didn't want paying. So, I tore up the cheque.
Bernard She was poor but she was honest?
Barbara That's right.
Bernard That's very complimentary. Am I really worth giving up a thousand euros for?
Barbara We'll have to find that out. It's funny, you know, you really turn me on.
Bernard In what way?
Barbara In every way. (*Moving closer to him*) Don't you fancy me at all?
Bernard Oh, very much. To tell the truth, I wasn't sure what I was letting myself in for. So, when I saw you, well — wow!
Barbara (*moving closer*) Wow?
Bernard Wait a minute! Look at me!
Barbara (*throatily*) That's all I want to do.
Bernard How old are you? What? Twenty-four?
Barbara Who's counting? Twenty-five. And all yours!

Act II, Scene 2   71

She starts to put her arms around him. Bernard strives, not very hard, to fend her off. He keeps glaring towards the terrace, fearing interruption

Bernard My wife ...
Barbara Jacqueline? She's lovely. But she cheats on you. (*Smoothing his lapels*) Before I came here, I didn't have a clue what you'd be like. (*Moving closer*) What you are like. What you do like. And you like me!
Bernard You think so?
Barbara I know it. The way you look at me. The huskiness in your voice.
Bernard I've got a cold.

Barbara reaches up to touch his lips with her fingers

Barbara Please, no more.

Bernard's defences are crumbling but he still keeps her at a distance

Bernard Well ...
Barbara Well, what? Say it!
Bernard Er, later, perhaps.
Barbara No! Now! (*She slips inside his arms and embraces him*) Tell me you want me!
Bernard (*trying to detach himself*) Look, why don't we have dinner first?

He manages to get to the service bell and rings for Marie-Louise

Barbara Why?
Bernard That will give me time to think this out.
Barbara What?
Bernard Whether it'd be right to let this opportunity slip.
Barbara (*embracing him again*) No! It would be wrong!

Barbara pulls Bernard's head down to kiss him

  Marie-Louise enters from the kitchen

Bernard, facing US, *does not see her. Marie-Louise takes a good look at them*

Marie-Louise Cor!

Bernard hurriedly detaches himself

    This bell ringing can be fun, can't it?
Bernard (*with asperity*) Not you again!
Marie-Louise Who else?
Bernard I told you to knock!
Marie-Louise You rang for me!
Bernard (*coming down to earth*) Oh. Yes. So I did. You can serve dinner now.
Marie-Louise I can't.
Bernard Why not?
Marie-Louise It's not done yet.
Bernard (*loudly*) All right, then when it is done!
Marie-Louise (*loudly*) All right, I will! Whenever that might be! (*Marching towards the kitchen door*) If you ask me, this dinner party is getting more and more peculiar! (*Turning to Bernard*) In fact, weird!

Marie-Louise exits

Barbara immediately approaches Bernard again

Bernard Do you know, she's right. I do feel weird!
Barbara (*clinging to him*) That's because you know I want you. (*She draws him into a kiss*)

Robert enters from the terrace, closing the doors behind him

Bernard notices Robert and quickly breaks away from Barbara

Robert So? How's it going then?
Bernard It's going fine. You're all right now, are you?
Robert Well, better. I'm not disturbing you?
Bernard No. I'm still waiting for my call.
Robert Right.

Robert leads Barbara back towards the terrace

    We'll leave you then.

Robert opens the glass doors for Barbara and we hear the coo of greeting voices off

    Barbara exits

Act II, Scene 2   73

Bernard I say!

Robert closes the door and comes back into the living-room

Robert Yes?
Bernard What was all that about with Madame Levée? Holding your tummy, moaning and groaning?
Robert Because, when I saw her, suddenly, in front of me — something came over me!
Bernard Well I could see that! What?
Robert Well, er, it's because I mistook her for ...
Bernard Who?
Robert Well, for someone else, that's all.
Bernard Yes, but for who else?
Robert Just a lady I used to know. Some time ago.
Bernard So?
Robert So, I was worried she might have said something, in front of, er ... (*He gestures vaguely after Barbara*)
Bernard I see. In front of Juliette?
Robert My wife. Yes. I'd be embarrassed if she got to know about this fling I once had. Little fling.
Bernard You do get around, don't you? But since you don't know her, how could she recognize you?
Robert Well, she couldn't but I thought she could. I mean, it was only afterwards that I realized it wasn't her.
Bernard Who?
Robert The Nicole I thought it was. I mean, that she wasn't the one I just mentioned to you.
Bernard Who was not called Levée?
Robert Exactly. And once I realized that, I began to feel better. A little better.
Bernard Now I understand. You lied, and you didn't want to be found out?
Robert Well, yes, I suppose so. Talking of which, tell me — it looked as though you and Juliette were quite close just now?
Bernard Me?
Robert Yes. (*Gesturing vaguely*) When I came in just now.
Bernard Meaning?
Robert (*with false bonhomie*) Don't deny it, I saw you, though I acted as though I'd seen nothing. Well? What's happening?
Bernard Oh, I don't know. It's not going too badly.
Robert Good. I'm pleased.
Bernard Only ...

Robert What?
Bernard Well, it's not — Look, put yourself in my place.
Robert How d'you mean?
Bernard I mean this sort of thing. It ought to be in a hotel. (*Pointedly*) Well, you know.
Robert I know? You mean the rue de Longchamp? Do you keep thinking about that?
Bernard What d'you think?
Robert I told you it was all finished between your wife and me. I don't need the place any more.
Bernard Well, that's what you say.
Robert No, really. Look, here's the keys. (*He takes a key ring from his pocket and hands it to Bernard*) Here, you have them.
Bernard Are you sure? (*Gesturing delicately*) That you want me to ——
Robert Do it! The lease runs for another six months. My room's on the third floor. You'll see, it's perfect. Very quiet, very peaceful, very discreet. Just stuff my things in a bag.
Bernard And what, give the bag to the concierge? For you to pick up?
Robert That's it! Then it's all done! I'm not at risk any more. Right?
Bernard (*spreading his hands*) All's well that ends well.
Robert (*emotionally*) Oh, thank you! I'm so glad! I must give you a hug!

Relieved, Robert takes Bernard by the shoulders and pulls him close

Marie-Louise enters from the kitchen

Marie-Louise (*looking at Bernard and Robert*) Well! Pardon me!

They both turn towards her. Robert still has one arm around Bernard

Bernard What is it?
Marie-Louise (*looking at them*) I didn't realize ...

Robert hurriedly drops his arm from around Bernard

Bernard Realize what?
Marie-Louise Well that you, er ... you and him ... (*Gesturing vaguely*) Nothing.
Bernard Look, when I haven't rung, I expect you to knock.
Marie-Louise To come in the living-room? I wish I hadn't now!
Bernard (*pointedly*) What do you want?
Marie-Louise (*pointedly*) To tell you it's ready.

Act II, Scene 2   75

Bernard What?
Marie-Louise To serve!
Bernard So?
Marie-Louise So nothing! If you want to be like that! (*As she goes to the kitchen; to herself*) Who's pairing up with who tonight, that's what I want to know!

Marie-Louise exits

Juliette comes in from the terrace

Bernard Ah, I'm glad you've come.
Juliette Me?
Bernard Yes. Bobby's just told me how terribly sorry he is for what happened.
Robert That's right. It was a sudden attack of malaria. If I don't take a dose of Malaprim immediately, well, I'm in trouble.
Bernard He tells me he doesn't even know where he is!
Juliette I realized it was something out of the ordinary.
Robert I do hope you'll excuse me.
Juliette Of course. Goodbye, Monsieur Regnier.
Robert Goodbye, Madame Levy.
Juliette (*frostily*) Levée. V—e—e.
Bernard (*to Juliette*) But aren't you going to stay for dinner?
Juliette No, I can't, really. My friends will be expecting me.
Barbara (*off*) Bobby, what are you doing?
Bernard I think your wife is after you.
Juliette Yes, I think she is.
Robert Well, I'd better go. (*To Juliette*) Once again, I'm so sorry.

Robert takes one last perplexed look at Juliette, shakes his head, then exits to the terrace

Juliette (*grimly*) He'll be sorry all right.
Bernard Calm down, Nicole.
Juliette Juliette, if you please! That's my name!
Bernard Yes, of course, Juliette.
Juliette (*moving towards the front door*) Well, goodbye.
Bernard But why leave now, when he still doesn't know you're you?
Juliette I must. Do you think I could sit through dinner with that liar opposite? Never!

Jacqueline enters from the terrace

Jacqueline I've got it! At last!
Bernard What?
Jacqueline (*to Juliette*) I've been racking my brains — it was outside a cinema somewhere — and now I remember!
Bernard (*dangerously*) What do you remember, dear?
Jacqueline You're the wife of …

Jacqueline gestures towards the terrace at the same time as realizing her mistake

Juliette (*looking straight at Jacqueline*) Of whom?
Bernard Yes? Whose wife?
Jacqueline (*trying to get out of it now*) Aah! No, of course not. I'm confusing you with someone else.
Juliette Yes. You must be.
Bernard Nicole will think that confusing people with other people is endemic in this household. (*To Juliette*) You've been confused quite a lot this evening.
Juliette Yes. Too much.
Bernard (*to Jacqueline*) Just a while ago, Bobby was convinced that Nicole was his wife. Can you believe that?
Jacqueline (*with a forced laugh*) Ridiculous, isn't it? But, you know, just for a moment, I did almost take you for …
Bernard For who?
Juliette Yes, who?
Jacqueline I've no idea. Someone I saw in a crowd.
Juliette That's probably it.
Bernard It's not really important, is it?
Jacqueline (*quickly*) No, not at all.

Bernard puts a friendly arm around Juliette

Bernard (*to Jacqueline*) Our visitor, unfortunately, can't stay for dinner.
Jacqueline I know! She told me. (*To Juliette*) We're very disappointed.
Juliette No more than I.
Jacqueline But I'm delighted to have met you, even if I did mix you up with — someone else.
Juliette (*smiling*) Oh, I'm not leaving because of that.
Bernard Yes, she has a previous engagement.
Juliette I'm afraid so.
Jacqueline Well then, we must say goodbye. Some other time perhaps?
Juliette Perhaps. Good-night.

Act II, Scene 2   77

Jacqueline and Juliette shake hands

Jacqueline exits to the terrace

Bernard My wife's not as good at lying as we are, is she?
Juliette Wait 'til I get that lying bugger of mine back home! Then he really will suffer. The apartment, the factory, the country house — they're all mine, you know?
Bernard As is your jewellery, of course.

Bernard takes the jewellery from his pocket and hands it to Juliette

Juliette That's right. He's never had to pay for anything. But he's going to pay dearly for what he's done now. Believe me!
Bernard Be reasonable. Life has its compensations.
Juliette It does? I'd like to know what? There's nothing can make up for all this.
Bernard Of course there is. (*He pats her hand gently*) You'll see.
Juliette Oh yes, I remember now. You know how to get your own back all right, don't you? (*Offering herself to him with open arms*) Do it then! Take me now! That way, we'll both get our own back.
Bernard (*taken aback*) Oh, come on now! You have never cheated!
Juliette True. But it's never too late.

She slips off her bolero and shakes out her hair, then pushes him towards the sofa

Bernard (*anxiously*) Look out! My wife might come in!
Juliette So what? She can't complain!
Bernard And Bobby?
Juliette He can make of it what he likes.
Bernard (*trying to extricate himself*) Come on now, be reasonable.
Juliette I am being reasonable. Not only am I compensating both of us, I'm having pleasure while saving my husband's life.
Bernard I suppose if you put it like that, it is reasonable. But not now!
Juliette When, then?
Bernard You're quite sure about this?
Juliette The best is always worth waiting for.
Bernard Do you know the rue de Longchamp?
Juliette I'll find it.
Bernard Number twenty-seven, third floor.
Juliette This evening?
Bernard No, I can't get away now. They'll suspect right away.
Juliette How about tomorrow then?

Bernard Five o'clock?
Juliette Fine. You've told me where and when. (*Moving close to him*) But don't tell me how, not yet! Let that be a surprise for me!

Juliette pulls Bernard down on the sofa and showers him with kisses

   Marie-Louise enters from the kitchen

Marie-Louise Whoops! Pardon me! Yet again!

Bernard hurriedly gets to his feet

   Marie-Louise makes a pointed about-turn and goes back to the kitchen

Juliette gets her bolero

Juliette This is the first time I've ever saved anyone's life.
Bernard I'm sure you'll find it an experience.
Juliette I will.

She shudders with passion. Bernard skips nimbly around her to get to the hall door

   Juliette follows Bernard, embraces him violently and then exits to the front door, just as Barbara comes in from the terrace

Bernard comes back into the middle of the living-room

Barbara I thought you'd like to know ... (*She displays another cheque*) He's given me the other half now.
Bernard That's kind of him.
Barbara But I'm not going to tear this cheque up.
Bernard Quite right. Once was enough.
Barbara It's not that. But he's paid me for going to bed with you and I told you, I don't want paying for that. I'll tear up the cheque — but not 'til afterwards.
Bernard There's no point. Let's face it. There's not going to be an afterwards.
Barbara Why not?
Bernard Because, between the two of us, it just isn't possible.
Barbara But it is. That's what I'm here for.
Bernard I respect your honesty. But let's say it is the intention that counts.

Act II, Scene 2   79

Barbara No. Unless you prefer me to tell him you know I'm not his wife.
Bernard That's blackmail.
Barbara Is that what they call it? If tonight's not convenient, how about tomorrow?
Bernard Ah. Tomorrow, I can't.
Barbara You're already booked?
Bernard You could say that.
Barbara How about Monday, then?
Bernard Do I have any choice?
Barbara No.
Bernard (*briskly*) Right. Monday. Five o'clock.

Barbara nods

Twenty-seven rue de Longchamp.

Barbara nods

Third floor.

Barbara leaps into his arms

Barbara It's going to be terrific fun! I'll tell Bobby it's all arranged!
Bernard No need to give him the address. He knows it.

Barbara goes back to the terrace, blowing him a kiss as she exits

Bernard rings the service bell

Well, what a Saturday!

Marie-Louise enters

Marie-Louise I say.
Bernard Yes?
Marie-Louise I want to tell you something.
Bernard Yes. What is it?
Marie-Louise Well ... (*She ogles him*) I find you very attractive too.
Bernard (*staggered*) No! That's it! I've had enough! Not you!
Marie-Louise I know I'm too good for you but as I seem to be the only one who hasn't made some kind of advance, I wouldn't like you to feel frustrated.

Bernard (*clutching his head*) This is really my day!

Jacqueline enters from the terrace

Jacqueline By the way, have you had it yet?
Bernard (*startled*) What?
Marie-Louise (*defensive*) No, not yet!
Jacqueline Your call.
Bernard Oh! Believe it or not, I've had two!
Jacqueline Good. (*Turning to Marie-Louise*) So can we eat at last?
Marie-Louise Whenever you like. But as it's all out there ... (*Gesturing towards the terrace*) I could do with a hand.
Bernard You know you only have to ask.

Bernard makes towards the kitchen but Jacqueline blocks him

Jacqueline No, let me help.
Marie-Louise It doesn't need three of us.

Marie-Louise eyes Bernard archly but Jacqueline gestures for him to stay

Jacqueline follows the disappointed Marie-Louise into the kitchen, just as Robert enters from the terrace

Robert (*jovially*) Well? What d'you say?
Bernard About what?
Robert (*delicately*) From what my wife told me, I, er, take it that there's been ... ?
Bernard Well, there's going to be.
Robert So I can stop worrying about having to look out for this psychopathic truck driver?
Bernard All over.
Robert Really?
Bernard Sure. (*Tapping his head*) It was all in here.
Robert What? (*It begins to dawn on him*) You mean there never was a truck?
Bernard I didn't say that. If you hadn't played your part, I only had to make one phone call. (*Meaningfully*) To my friends in Marseilles.
Robert (*staring at him*) You would really have done it, wouldn't you?
Bernard If I were you, I'd just forget it.

Jacqueline enters from the kitchen

Act II, Scene 2

Jacqueline Right, everything's ready. We can go and sit down.
Bernard Good. I'll uncork the wine.

Bernard goes off into the kitchen

Jacqueline Do you know, I nearly tripped up just now?
Robert In what way?
Jacqueline I nearly blurted out to Bernard that your wife was here.
Robert She is here.
Jacqueline Your real wife.
Robert My real wife? What are you talking about? You're crazy.
Jacqueline No, I'm not. I'm certain she was the one I saw you with, coming out of the cinema that time.
Robert Never, on my life! She was like her, yes. But you're mixing them up. My wife is much plumper, much taller, and much fairer. And she always wears earrings. Mind you, I know what you mean, even though I know her a lot better than you, I believed that myself for a bit. And anyway, she's not called Nicole Levy. Levée.
Jacqueline I know that, stupid!
Robert So there you are. You were confused. I was confused. It was all very confusing.

Jacqueline looks at him for a moment

Jacqueline Good. That's that, then. Now we can take up where we left off.
Robert (*taken aback*) Do you think we can?

The doorbell rings

Jacqueline Well, if he's going to start cheating on me now, I don't see why I should deprive myself.
Robert But we can't! Didn't I tell you I had to give up the room? The lease ran out.
Jacqueline What difference does that make? There are plenty of others for rent. So for next Saturday, you can go and find another. I'm counting on you.

Jacqueline smiles sweetly as she goes back to the terrace

Robert is struck dumb

Marie-Louise enters

Marie-Louise Did someone ring the front door?
Robert I think so.

The doorbell rings again

Marie-Louise goes to answer the front door

Juliette rushes in to the living-room, followed by Marie-Louise

Marie-Louise Oh, right! Changed your mind, have you? Don't worry about me!
Juliette No, I forgot my bag.

She rushes straight to the sofa where she left it

Marie-Louise Well, you've got it back now.

Juliette looks through her bag

Marie-Louise goes grumpily back to the kitchen

Juliette has hardly noticed Robert, who is more confident now

Robert Well, hello again, Madame Levée.
Juliette (*glaring at him*) Stop behaving like an idiot.
Robert What?
Juliette I know everything.

Juliette starts towards the front door

Robert (*appealing*) Nicole.

She stops, turns, then gives him such a ferocious look he knows the game is up

  Juliette!
Juliette I know all about it, and I mean everything! I'm telling you though, I'll get my own back, you just wait and see.

She goes to the hall doorway

Robert (*crying from the heart*) But, Juliette!
Juliette (*with one last look at him*) No! Just don't say anything! There's nothing more to say!

Act II, Scene 2

Juliette exits through the hall, slamming the front door behind her

Robert (*devastated*) Oh my God! (*He clutches his head, trying to work out everything that has just happened*)

Bernard enters from the kitchen, carrying some bottles of wine

Bernard Here we are then. All right?
Robert No. I've just been thinking about something.
Bernard What's that?
Robert I was wondering if, by any chance, you were thinking you might have it off with that Nicole Levy?
Bernard Levée. É-e. What if I did?
Robert Well, I didn't mention it at the time but these drivers, you know, the ones who skid their trucks so dangerously — I might be able to get hold of one myself.
Bernard (*chuckling*) You!
Robert And even if I couldn't — I could always rent a truck myself!
Bernard You can't be serious.
Robert Find out. I suggest though, if you value your health, you'll stay away from Juliette.

The two men engage in a brief mime as to just which Juliette they are talking about. They stare at each other, challengingly

Marie-Louise enters, carrying a tray containing serving dishes

Marie-Louise Well, don't hang about! Dinner's being served! What are you waiting for?

Robert points a finger of silent warning and then moves off to the terrace

Bernard, thoughtful, is about to follow when he is halted by Marie-Louise, who gives him a monstrous wink. Bernard looks at her, startled

Marie-Louise How about Tuesday?

The Lights fade to Black-out

CURTAIN

FURNITURE AND PROPERTY LIST

ACT I
Scene 1

On stage: Curtains at sliding glass doors
Mirror
Service bell with a string
Sofa. *On it*: cushions
Chair
Side table. *On it*: telephone, diary
Well-stocked drinks cabinet. *In it*: glasses, vermouth, whisky, malt, rye and other assorted drinks

Off stage: Hat, handbag (**Marie-Louise**)
Bunch of flowers (**Robert**)

Personal: **Jacqueline**: watch
Marie-Louise: watch
Bernard: Rolex watch, mobile phone, diary
Robert: notebook, pen

Scene 2

Re-set: Flowers in a vase on side table

Off stage: Ice bucket with opened bottle of champagne (**Marie-Louise**)
Frozen veal, frozen lamb stroganoff (**Marie-Louise**)

ACT II
Scene 1

On stage: Flowers in a vase

Off stage: Handbag (**Juliette**)
Ice bucket, bottle of champagne (**Bernard**)

Personal: **Juliette**: rings (including a wedding ring), earrings

Furniture and Property List

Scene 2

Off stage: Damp cloth, bottles of wine (**Bernard**)
Tray (**Marie-Louise**)

Personal: **Barbara**: two cheques
Robert: key ring

LIGHTING PLOT

Property fittings required: nil

ACT I, SCENE 1

To open: Interior lighting

Cue 1   **Bernard** moves towards the kitchen door   (Page 26)
          Fade to black-out

ACT I, SCENE 2

To open: Interior lighting, evening; sparkling backdrop reflecting the lights of Montparnasse

Cue 2   **Bernard** smiles with satisfaction   (Page 32)
          Fade to black-out

ACT II, SCENE 1

To open: Interior lighting, evening; sparkling backdrop reflecting the lights of Montparnasse

Cue 3   **Robert** heads to the terrace. **Bernard** halts him   (Page 62)
          Fade to black-out

ACT II, SCENE 2

To open: Interior lighting, evening; sparkling backdrop reflecting the lights of Montparnasse

Cue 4   **Marie-Louise**: "How about Tuesday?"   (Page 83)
          Fade to black-out

EFFECTS PLOT

ACT I

Cue 1	**Bernard**: "Bye." *Front door closes*	(Page 2)
Cue 2	**Bernard** mimes welcoming a guest. Pause *Front doorbell rings*	(Page 6)
Cue 3	**Bernard**: "… Don't let me down." *Front doorbell rings*	(Page 7)
Cue 4	**Marie-Louise** adjusts her hat in the mirror *Front doorbell rings*	(Page 7)
Cue 5	**Marie-Louise** exits *Front door slams*	(Page 8)
Cue 6	**Robert**: "… I never really had a choice." *A noise sounds from above*	(Page 20)
Cue 7	**Robert**: "Are you giving me orders?" *Front door opens*	(Page 21)
Cue 8	**Bernard** goes to the front door *Front door closes*	(Page 23)
Cue 9	To open Scene 2 *Front doorbell rings*	(Page 27)

ACT II

Cue 10	**Bernard**: "That's very touching." *Doorbell rings*	(Page 48)
Cue 11	**Bernard**: "Like this." *Doorbell rings twice*	(Page 59)
Cue 12	**Bernard**: "Or with a gun. Pouf, pouf!" *Doorbell rings*	(Page 62)

Cue 13	**Bernard**: "Otherwise —Pouf, pouf!" *Doorbell rings*	(Page 62)
Cue 14	**Robert**: "Do you think we can?" *Doorbell rings*	(Page 81)
Cue 15	**Robert**: "I think so." *Doorbell rings*	(Page 82)
Cue 16	**Juliette** exits *Front door slams*	(Page 83)

www.ingramcontent.com/pod-product-compliance
Ingram Content Group UK Ltd.
Pitfield, Milton Keynes, MK11 3LW, UK
UKHW021844210426
5322IPUK00022B/450